CW00543672

Cup Kings
Manchester City
1956

©1999

Published by
Over the Moon
Liverpool

Book design by
March Design
Liverpool

Printed by
GZ Printek
Spain

All rights reserved. No part of this publication may be
reproduced, stored in a retrieval system, or transmitted
in any form or by any means, electronic, mechanical,
photocopying, recording or otherwise, without prior
permission from the publisher.

ISBN 1 872568 66 1

The authors wish to acknowledge the assistance given
by Ken Barnes, Roy Clarke, Bert Trautmann, Phil Noble
and the Manchester Evening News. Without their help,
this book would not have been possible.

Cup Kings
Manchester City
1956

Compiled by
John Maddox
David Saffer
Peter Robinson

overthe**moon**

Foreword
by Roy Clarke

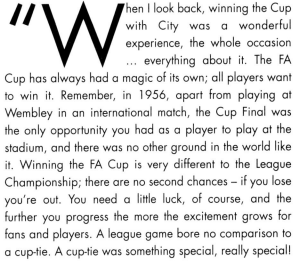

"When I look back, winning the Cup with City was a wonderful experience, the whole occasion ... everything about it. The FA Cup has always had a magic of its own; all players want to win it. Remember, in 1956, apart from playing at Wembley in an international match, the Cup Final was the only opportunity you had as a player to play at the stadium, and there was no other ground in the world like it. Winning the FA Cup is very different to the League Championship; there are no second chances – if you lose you're out. You need a little luck, of course, and the further you progress the more the excitement grows for fans and players. A league game bore no comparison to a cup-tie. A cup-tie was something special, really special!

Playing for Manchester City was a wonderful experience.The camaraderie was fantastic and you would not believe the banter in the dressing room prior to a game. We were all on the same money so there was no room for petty jealousy; when you joined you knew what you'd be on; you didn't expect any more. Friends made on the playing field were friends for life. We shared something special and today, over forty years on, members of the team still meet regularly to talk over old times and watch their favourite team play.

Sadly, not all the 1956 team are with us and this book is a tribute to Don Revie, Joe Hayes, Dave Ewing and of course, Les McDowall whose inspired management resulted in that most precious of honours – the FA Cup!

Roy Clarke

Manchester City in the FA Cup

The FA Cup has been called the greatest club competition in world football. With the growth in importance of European club competitions, the status of the domestic tournament has been somewhat diminished but to English fans, at least, there is still an undeniable magic about a competition which, season after season, pits the minnows of football against the giants, giving hope each year to supporters that their team might be the one to make it through to the final encounter under the twin towers of Wembley.

Supporters of Manchester City have plenty of reasons to look forward to the Cup. After all, in spite of the club's bizarre ability to lose its sense of direction at critical times, its FA Cup record is amongst the best, winning the trophy four times, in 1904, 1934, 1956 and 1969, and losing as finalists four times in 1926, 1933, 1955 and 1981.

Their first Cup venture was as Ardwick FC in 1890-91. They played in the first qualifying round on 4 October 1890 in front of a crowd of 4000 at Hyde Road and destroyed Liverpool Stanley by the grand score of 12-0. Everybody in the forward line scored, with former Bolton Wanderer Davie Weir hitting in three goals. With such a resounding victory you might have thought that Ardwick were raring to go into the next round. Not a bit of it. With a glimpse of the eccentricity that has become part and parcel of the club, they inexplicably withdrew from the competition a fortnight later when they were due to face the might of Halliwell FC!

In 1894-95, as Manchester City they did not bother to enter the competition and the following season, rather than face the bother of rearranging a League game against Darwen on 12 October, they again withdrew from the competition having been drawn against Oswaldtwistle Rovers.

The next few years were uneventful until 1901, when they faced a very strong Preston North End side. The first meeting on 25 January was abandoned in extra time and the replay, four days later, ended in a 0-0 draw. The Blues then shook the football world by winning 4-2 at Deepdale, with 'Stockport' Smith grabbing a hat-trick. At the end of the season, City were relegated.

North End exacted their revenge the following season by winning at home by 3-1, but City did not have to wait too long for their first taste of Cup glory. The 1903-04 season saw the team promoted back to the First Division and triumphing in the FA Cup for the first time. Sunderland were the first victims, beaten 3-2 at Hyde Road with goals from Turnbull (2) and Billy Gillespie. Next Woolwich Arsenal were walloped 2-0 on their own turf, Turnbull scoring again and outside-left 'Tabby' Booth getting the other. Middlesbrough forced a goalless draw at Hyde Road but the Blues won comfortably at Ayresome Park, Turnbull, Gillespie and George Livingstone all scoring in a 3-1 victory.

Heady days indeed! For the semi-final, City was drawn against Sheffield Wednesday in a game to be played at Everton's Goodison Park. A crowd of 53,000 turned up on a

Manchester City 1
Hillman
McMahon
Burgess
Frost
Hynds
Ashworth
Meredith
Livingstone
Gillespie
Turnbull
Booth

Bolton Wanderers 0
Davies
Brown
Struthers
Clifford
Greenhalgh
Freebairn
Stokes
Marsh
Yenson
White
Taylor

soggy afternoon on 19 March, the City fans aware that Wednesday should be afforded great respect as they were indeed the League champions from the previous campaign.

But the City manager, Tom Maley, was a football thinker and he had reasoned that to upset the Owls, the Blues must attack from the start. This they did and took the lead after 21 minutes through the Welsh wizard Billy Meredith hitting the Wednesday crossbar and Billy Gillespie seizing on the loose ball to force it home. Meredith created the second goal before the interval. His accurate cross was whipped past the Owls' keeper, Jack Lyall – later a City player – by Turnbull.

It was the same combination that brought the third and decisive goal in the second half. The Blues were on their way to the Final which would be against Bolton Wanderers at the Crystal Palace (not to be confused with Selhurst Park). Even then, the FA favoured London as a venue for big games, irrespective of how far the supporters of clubs had to travel. Although the ground could accommodate more than 100,000 people, it was fortunate that a considerably smaller crowd attended – 61,374 – as the viewing facilities were far from satisfactory. A journalist for the Athletics News sports paper hovered above the venue in a balloon.

The only goal of the game was a controversial one which greatly upset the Bolton fans. What did matter was the referee's opinion, and he was firm in his decision that when Billy Meredith took possession of the ball he was not offside. Livingstone was the provider and Meredith went round full-back Robert Struthers and scored.

Bolton managed to dump the Blues out of the Cup the following season and there again followed a series of mediocre years. City had lost the services of their manager and a large number of players (17) were suspended and fined through the overpayments scandal of 1906, with 12 players eventually ordered to be transferred away from Hyde Road. In addition, Meredith had been suspended for allegedly offering a bribe to an Aston Villa player to throw a match. In 1912-13 there came further trouble for City when a crowd invasion caused an FA Cup tie against Sunderland to be abandoned at Hyde Road. The root of the problem was sheer overcrowding, many of the fans not counted in the 41,709 official attendance, having broken down gates to get in. The Blues lost the replayed game at Sunderland 0-2.

There was a respectable Cup run the following season with City beating Fulham (2-0) and Spurs (2-1) at Hyde Road before gaining a 2-1 victory at Ewood Park against Blackburn. In March, City played a series of three matches against Sheffield United. The first ended goalless at Hyde Road, as did the replay at Bramall Lane, then the teams had a trek to Villa Park for the second replay which the Blades won by a solitary strike.

There was, of course, no FA Cup football during the Great War and City had little success until 1923-24, when they reached the semi-finals, playing eight games in all including three against Halifax Town. Nottingham Forest were the first to be ousted, Frank Roberts and Horace Barnes scoring in a 2-1 Maine Road win (the club had switched to this new venue the previous summer), then Halifax held the Blues to a 2-2 draw in Manchester. A scoreless draw followed at The Shay, but City were not too unhappy at the choice of venue for the second replay ... all the way to Old Trafford! There they overcame the Yorkshire side 3-0.

A trip to Brighton was next on the agenda and the sea air obviously did City a power

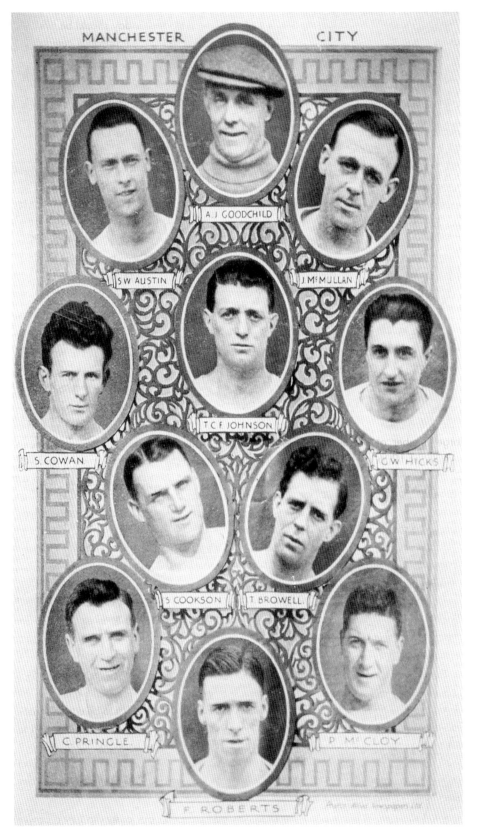

MANCHESTER CITY

A.J GOODCHILD

S.W AUSTIN

J. McMULLAN

T.C.F. JOHNSON

S. COWAN

O.W HICKS

S COOKSON

T. BROWELL

C. PRINGLE

P. McCLOY

F. ROBERTS

The Manchester City Cup team of 1926. They lost 1-0 to Bolton in a hard fought Final after scoring 31 goals en route to Wembley.

of good. Over 24,000 people squeezed into the ground to see the Blues romp home 5-1, and a major talking point was the appearance of 49-years old Billy Meredith who scored a goal with the help of the Brighton keeper.

On 8 March, a gate of of 76,166 squashed into the new stadium in Manchester to see Cardiff City force a 0-0 scoreline and, four days later, it was the ageless Meredith who supplied the cross that Browell forced into the Cardiff net at Ninian Park for the winner.

It was time now for the semi-final, the Blues' opponents being Newcastle United in a game played at St Andrews in Birmingham. This time it was disappointment for City fans. The Magpies totally outplayed the Blues, running out 2-0 winners to face Aston Villa who they beat by the same scoreline to take the trophy to Tyneside.

However, two years later, City did make the final but it was a season with more than a tinge of sadness for the Blues were not only defeated at Wembley but relegated as well. The Cup-run itself was memorable both for the number of goals City scored and some of the astonishing attendances.

The opening tie was at Crystal Palace against the famous amateur team Corinthians, who surprised most people by securing a 3-3 draw. The dependable Roberts equalized the score with a few minutes remaining, the earlier goals coming from Sammy Cookson and George Hicks. Hicks was again on the scoring list in the Maine Road replay, the Blues coolly going through to the next round 4-0.

In the fourth round, a crowd of 74,789 watched a 4-0 demolition of Huddersfield Town but the most remarkable game in the competition was against Crystal Palace at Maine Road. The final score was 11-4 to City who were seven goals clear by the interval. Palace rallied and they disturbed the complacency the Blues were showing by pulling four goals back, but this only spurred City on and they scored a further four by the final whistle. The scoring spree continued away at Clapton Orient in the sixth round. This time City only managed a mere six against one in reply but, again, it was a most convincing display.

If there is only one thing better than beating Manchester United at Wembley. it's beating them in a semi-final and denying them the chance of getting there, which is precisely what City did at Sheffield United's Bramall Lane ground.

The Blues governed the game, taking the lead as early as the 14th minute. Hicks crossed from a corner kick and Browell rose to head the ball home. United complained (what's new?) that Browell had pushed a player to get to the ball and that the ball had not crossed the line. The referee treated these moans with the contempt they deserved.

It was 1-0 at the break, with City becoming evermore the dominant team. The woodwork saved the Reds on several occasions, but they went further behind after 75 minutes, again through a Hicks-Browell combination and, two minutes later, it was Roberts' turn to get on the scoresheet when his seemingly innocuous effort was deflected into the net by goalkeeper Alf Steward. So it was Wembley here we come, for the first City visit to the national stadium.

En route to the final City had scored 31 goals in six games, conceding eight. Sadly, the high hopes of the supporters were dashed when Bolton avenged their 1904 defeat in front of a 91,547 crowd, winning by the only goal of the game.

It was an excellent cup final with little between the two sides who gave their all, a credit to Lancashire. The Bolton hero was their goalkeeper, Dick Pym, who came to the Wanderers' rescue on more than one occasion. Jimmy McMullan, who had arrived from Partick Thistle the previous February, constantly covered the length of the pitch and was a permanent thorn in Bolton's side.

The decisive goal came with just thirteen minutes to go. Welsh international Vizard cut the ball back from the left wing straight into David Jack's path, who had timed his run to perfection. Jimmy Goodchild in the City goal had no chance.

So the Blues were defeated this time around but on the way to the final they had provided wonderful entertainment for their supporters. Sadly, their league performance was less heart-warming and relegation had been hanging over the club. Despite a 2-1 win over Leeds United at Maine Road, they were beaten 2-3 at Newcastle in the final game of the season and the Blues were vanquished to the Second Division.

After the 1926 final, the club continued to under-achieve although in 1931-32, they managed to reach the semi-finals. Once more an ambitious First Division club, they had made some shrewd signings with players such as Eric Brook, Fred Tilson and Ernie Toseland joining them.

The third round at Millwall started with an immediate set-back for the Blues when the home team scored after just 60 seconds, After a thrilling match, City emerged as 3-2 winners to face Brentford at Maine Road in the fourth round. A crowd of 56,190 turned up to watch the Blues massacre the Londoners 6-1 with Tilson scoring a hat-trick, Eric Brook hitting home two penalties, and Halliday completing the rout.

Derby County were the next opponents, again at Maine Road, and over 62,000 turned up for the tie which City won 3-0. A close tussle with Bury followed at Gigg Lane – close in the long run, that is. City were four goals to the good by the interval, courtesy of Toseland (2), Halliday and Sammy Cowan, but Bury fought back tenaciously and put three past City keeper Len Langford. At the end, anyone but a City fan felt sorry for Bury.

March 12th saw the semi-final clash against Arsenal at Villa Park, which was to become one of City's lucky cup venues in later years. Not this time, though. Arsenal scored the only goal of the game through their outside-left, Cliff Bastin. City full-back Billy Felton was deemed responsible for the goal and swiftly transferred to Spurs.

So that season ended on a flat note but the Blues were to reach the twin towers of Wembley in each of the subsequent years. It was Wilf Wild's first season in charge of the team, combining the manager's role with the secretary's tasks and, while the League form was poor, the Cup run gave a great deal of encouragement to those who followed the club's fortunes.

The third round saw City playing out a 1-1 draw in a quagmire at Gateshead. Back in Manchester, the replay was virtually one-way traffic, the Blues romping home 9-0. Tilson secured a hat–trick, there were two goals from Cowan, and the rest came from Matty Barrass, Matt Busby, Jimmy McMullan and Brook.

Walsall were summarily dismissed 2-0 from the competition at Moss Side in front of a crowd of over 52,000. Then followed a full-house game at Burnden Park against old cup adversaries Bolton. Brook scored three goals in the 4-0 victory which also marked Alec Herd's first FA Cup game for the Blues.

FA Cup Final
Wembley 1933

Manchester City 0
Langford
Cann
Dale
Busby
Cowan
Bray
Toseland
Marshall
Herd
McMullan
Brook

Everton 3
Sagar
Cook
Cresswell
Britton
White
Thomson
Geldard
Dunn
Dean
Johnson
Stein

13

Another red rose scalp followed. A short trip to Burnley culminated in another Blues win, this time by the only goal of the match with the reward of a semi-final place against Derby to be played across the Pennines in Huddersfield. A strong start saw City score the first two goals and, with 20 minutes left McMullan hit home a third. Derby were stung into action and pulled two goals back in the following four minutes but they had left it too late and the Blues were through to Wembley to face a third Lancashire club, Everton.

In the first Cup Final in which the players wore numbers, City goalkeeper Langford had an attack of Wembley nerves, Faced by a formidable Everton attack, Langford dropped a cross and allowed Everton to take advantage through Jimmy Stein. The City keeper committed another major error early in the second half when he again dropped a ball played in by Cliff Britton, who later managed Everton for eight years. This time Dixie Dean power-headed the ball into the net. Jimmy Dunn scored Everton's third from a Geldard looping centre.

So it was another disappointment for City fans. It did not help that former Blue hero Tommy Johnson was in the Evertonians' ranks. However, skipper Sam Cowan promised everybody that the club would return the following season and return is exactly what they did, this time successfully. Since Christmas 1933, the legendary Frank Swift had gained and kept a place in the City goalmouth and his remarkable skill gave the rest of the team a vast amount of confidence.

The home gates at Maine Road in the Cup were quite astonishing, the lowest being 49,042 in a replay, the highest being the club's record attendance – 84,569.

The first opponents of this season were again Lancastrian in the form of Blackburn Rovers; a crowd of 54,336 attending to see a 3-0 City win with goals from Toseland (2) and Brook. There followed a trek to Hull City, where the home side astonished all but themselves by grabbing an equaliser with a few minutes left to make the score 2-2. This time, a goal from Herd accompanied Brook's strike. The replay at Maine Road resulted in a solid 4-1 victory.

The Blues helped to set an attendance record at Hillsborough which still stands today. when they played Sheffield Wednesday in the fifth round in front of nearly 73,000 supporters. At least one spectator was killed in the crush, an unheeded warning of the dangers of over-crowding.

The match itself was a stalemate. Wednesday's Rimmer opened the scoring but Alec Herd equalised. Scottish international Neil Dewar then gave Wednesday a further lead but Herd again saved the Blues' bacon and the Owls had to come to Moss Side, where they were beaten 2-0 with long-range goals from both Tilson and Marshall.

The sixth round brought Stoke City and Stanley Matthews to Manchester for that record attendance, and Eric Brook was the hero that day when his somewhat speculative effort from the right touchline sailed over the Stoke keeper's head to take the Blues into the semi-finals. Once again, the game was played at Huddersfield (it would not have been fair to have held it at Villa Park seeing that our opponents were Aston Villa!). City went at the Midlanders from the outset and absolutely mesmerised them, building a four goal lead by the interval thanks to Toseland, Tilson (2) and Herd. Tilson doubled his tally in the second half before Astley scored a consolation goal for Villa in what was one of the most one-sided semi-finals ever. So it was on to Wembley to face Portsmouth.

FA Cup Final
Wembley
28 April 1934

Manchester City 2
Swift
Barnett
Dale
Busby
Cowan
Bray
Toseland
Marshall
Tilson
Herd
Brook

Portsmouth 1
Gilfillan
Mackie
Smith W
Nichol
Allen
Thackeray
Worrall
Smith J
Weddle
Easson
Rutherford

The 1934 team gather for an informal photograph at the Palace Hotel, Southport, before the Cup Final.

The winning 1934 team.

City had prepared for the the final at the seaside resort of Southport before travelling to a hotel near Epping Forest. The team were in good spirits, confident that this was going to be their year but it was the south coast side that took the lead within 30 minutes. John Weddle cleared Sam Cowan's head and found Sep Rutherford, the left-winger. His shot in turn was touched by Frank Swift in goal but even Frank's giant reach wasn't long enough to prevent the ball from entering the net. Swift was quite distraught, but Tilson comforted him in the dressing-room at the interval and assured him that he would put a couple of goals into the Portsmouth net in the second half.

Which is exactly what he did! Tilson and Brook changed places, Tilson cut inside, and scored with precision to level matters. Play swung from end to end, Swift at one point making a brilliant save, and it was not until the last five minutes that Tilson made good his promise and cracked in the winner from a Toseland pass. The tension was too much for Swift, the young keeper fainting when the final whistle went!

During the remaining years in the 1930's, the Blues twice reached the sixth round, losing in their championship season 1936-37 to Millwall – and beating them the following year before losing to Aston Villa. The best result of these two series of cup games was a 5-0 win at Bolton, the mercurial Peter Doherty the mastermind behind this resounding victory.

There was no recognised FA Cup competition during World War Two, and the years that followed were barren ones for City until 1954-55. That was the year when manager Les McDowall introduced his 'Revie Plan' which was based on the style of play practised by the Hungarian national team.

City's third round opponents were Derby County. The trip to Derby saw the Blues ending up 3-1 winners thanks to goals from Ken Barnes, little Joe Hayes and a Don Revie penalty.

And what a draw the next round proved to be: City v Manchester United! Maine Road was crammed with 74,723 spectators. Local pride was at stake and, in a bad-tempered match in which United's Allenby Chilton was sent off, Hayes and Revie provided the goals which took the Blues through to the fifth round. City had already beaten their local rivals at Maine Road 3-2, and a fortnight later were to compound United's misery by slamming in five goals at Old Trafford without reply!

The fifth round drew the Blues against a tricky Luton Town. It was a gluepot pitch but City overcame it and progressed thanks to two goals from left-winger Roy Clarke, the first provided by Paddy Fagan. It was a relief to Les McDowall that the team had come through such poor conditions successfully.

Next port of call was St Andrews where City had to face Birmingham City. The game proved to be a real struggle and the travelling Maine Road punters were ecstatic when Johnny Hart, that grand club servant, hit in the winning goal past Gil Merrick.

So it was back to Birmingham, this time to Villa Park, to face Sunderland in the semi-final. Again the playing conditions were difficult and City was without Hart who had broken a leg in a league match at Huddersfield. In a way this eased a problem, for the manager had just signed the Scottish wizard Bobby Johnstone and Hart's injury gave him the opportunity to find a place for him.

Roy Clarke headed the only goal of the game from a delivery by Joe Hayes, ensuring a Wembley trip for City fans. Unfortunately, Clarke was injured later in the game and a further injury in a league game caused him to miss the final, leaving him bitterly disappointed.

Newcastle United were City's opponents at Wembley, a side full of talented players including the clever George Hannah who would sign for City some years later. The worst possible scenario faced City. After a mere 45 seconds, a Len White corner kick was headed home off the crossbar by Jackie Milburn. Then, 18 minutes later Jimmy Meadows was helped from the pitch after damaging his cruciate ligaments as his studs caught in the turf. No subs in those days, of course, and it meant the end of Jimmy's playing career.

Captain Roy Paul rallied the troops in his inimitable way and Johnstone equalised with a marvellous header from ten yards but, sadly, it wasn't enough. As other teams have discovered, playing with ten men at Wembley is not an ideal situation and, after 53 minutes, Bobby Mitchell scored United's second goal from the narrowest of angles, leaving Bert Trautmann angry with himself. George Hannah slammed in the third Geordie goal six minutes later, and the door to success was firmly shut in the Blues' faces.

Bert Trautmann has vivid memories of his first Wembley appearance. " You had goose pimples on your skin when they stood up and sang 'Abide with Me'. As a player, the goose pimples were real; you're so small with so many people around you, it was magnificent. I think I was one of the first foreigners to play in a Cup Final, the feeling inside you … you couldn't describe it … tremendous. I remember staying for ten days in Eastbourne at the Grange Hotel for 'special training' before going by coach to Wembley. We were the first team to walk out at Wembley in tracksuits!

Up till half time, we were in control, but we lost Jimmy Meadows and, as the second half went on, they grew stronger. They had a good forward line that included Jackie Milburn. He scored one with his head in the first minute; he'd never headed one like that before, we couldn't believe it. You can play till you're absolutely exhausted, both mentally and physically, you're drained of everything, but even exhausted players absorb defeat. Of course there were tears because you never know if you'll get the chance to go back again, but I remember Roy Paul saying 'We'll be back!' It was in City's history losing a Cup Final and going back next season. In the end, though, I had achieved something lots of players never experienced.'

Ken Barnes remembers the atmosphere of playing Cup football at that time: 'In our day there were only two things to win, the Championship and the Cup. We were quite happy just to stay in the First Division because there were so many good sides around, if you won the Cup it was a bonus. In Lancashire alone, we had Manchester United, Blackpool, Bolton, Burnley, Preston, Liverpool and Everton within sixty miles of us. The games were always a sell-out with crowds between 40,000 and 70,000. The atmosphere was unbelievable.

In the semi finals against Sunderland, the pitch was in a terrible state, there were pools of water everywhere and you couldn't run with the ball; it just got stuck in the mud. During the game, Sunderland's centre forward, Len Shackleton, countered this by scooping the ball up and juggling it as he ran before attempting a volley. I thought you cheeky so and so! As for the Final, of course we were disappointed. Jackie Milburn headed their first; Roy Paul was marking him and couldn't believe it because Milburn had never headed a goal like that in his life. We equalised but after Jimmy Meadows got injured that was it really, they came more into the game and it became very difficult for us.'

Manchester City 1

Trautmann

Meadows

Little

Barnes

Ewing

Paul

Spurdle

Hayes

Revie

Johnstone

Fagan

Newcastle United 3

Simpson

Cowell

Batty

Scoular

Stokoe

Casey

White

Milburn

Keeble

Hannah

Mitchell

To Roy Clarke, the Final was a bitter personal disappointment, missing out through injury. The semi-final was a different matter. 'Before the semi-final against Sunderland, the referee was worried about the state of the pitch due to all the rain. The police, however, were more concerned about the fans and the fact that if the match was postponed, the rescheduled game would be on the same night as another game in the city. After much discussion between the officials, the game went ahead. I had a mixed game emotionally because, after scoring the only goal of the match I got carried off, which put me out of the Final. There's a picture of my goal where in the background you can clearly see the supporters' faces in the stand; they have no expression at all. That's because the ball was nearly on the ground when I headed it and it took ages to go in. Apart from myself Johnny Hart missed out on Wembley due to a broken leg, but we were allowed to stay at the team hotel. On the day, Johnny and I went down to Wembley ahead of the team. When we arrived at the players' entrance, the stewards wouldn't let either of us in. We couldn't believe it. We had to wait for the team coach to arrive before being allowed inside; we watched the game from the bench. Against Newcastle we were forced to play Bill Spurdle out of position, in defence, after Jimmy Meadows was injured. We suffered and it definitely affected the balance of the side. At the end, everyone was terribly disappointed but Roy Paul came into his own and told us in no uncertain fashion that we'd be back next year. He was right.'

There is no need to dwell on the glory of 1956 as that is what this book is all about. Suffice to say that, despite having a goalkeeper playing for the latter stages of the game with a broken neck, Manchester City excited all of those who watched the match with their attractive style of play.

The triumph of 1956 was followed by years in the Cup wilderness. The following season, City again faced Newcastle. A draw at St James's was followed by the Blues stylishly losing 5-4 at home in an extra-time replay having been ahead 3-0!

1960-61 was also an odd cup experience. There were three games against Cardiff City which the Blues eventually won 2-0 – at Highbury. The following round was at Luton in torrential rain. The pitch turned into a morass and the referee cruelly abandoned the game, much to the chagrin of Denis Law. Denis had cracked in six goals to make the final scoreline 6-2, but his place in the record books was erased by the referee's decision. To make matters worse, Denis scored again when the tie was played later, only for City to lose 3-1.

The winter of 1962-63 was utterly dreadful. Severe frost set in around Boxing Day and eradicated all football for weeks. The Blues flew to Dublin to play Burnley in a friendly just for match practice and, when the FA Cup games finally got underway, City played three rounds in ten days, beginning on March 6th. Alex Harley scored in all three games, the Blues beating both Walsall and Bury 1-0 before defeat at the hands of Norwich City, 2-1.

But the glory days were on the way. The inspired partnership of Joe Mercer and Malcolm Allison saw the Blues back in the top flight in their very first season as well as reaching the sixth round of the Cup, which went to two replays against Everton. These were days when Glyn Pardoe was still playing up front before his full-back conversion and he scored at Blackpool in the third round to win a Maine Road replay in front of over 52,000 fans. Johnny Crossan, Mike Summerbee and Mike Doyle scored in the 3-1 victory.

Summerbee was also on target against Grimsby Town in the next round with John

Cockerill's own goal sealing defeat for the Fishermen. The fifth round pitched the Blues against Leicester City in the first of what would be many cup encounters over the next few seasons. Two goals from Neil Young took the game to a replay at Filbert Street, and the same player secured the only strike of the game to take City into the sixth round.

The initial game against Everton, and also the replay, ended goalless although they were full of excitement and watched by a total of 123,383 fans! The second replay at Molyneux proved too much for City who also had promotion on their minds. Goals from Derek Temple and Fred Pickering destroyed City's chances of meeting Manchester United in the semi-final.

The Blues again reached the sixth round the following season – again meeting Leicester City on the way – and the Foxes then knocked us out in 1967-68 in the fourth round although there was one small consolation that year with Manchester City ending up as League Champions!

The following season, a Francis Lee penalty despatched Luton from the contest in the third round. In the next round, an excellent game at Newcastle ended goalless. Young Tommy Booth marked Welsh international Wyn Davies out of the game and helped ensure that the Tynesiders were forced to travel to Moss Side for a replay. City's phenomenal home support came out in force to witness Neil Young and newcomer Bobby Owen score the goals that took the Blues through to fifth round. The two games were watched by 115,624 spectators.

City's next opponents were Blackburn but a bizarre sequence of events saw the game postponed more than 20 times because of either the state of the pitch or the 'flu epidemic that swept through the Rovers' ranks. When the tie was eventually played, it was one of easiest games the Blues had that season. Both Lee and Tony Coleman scored twice as City romped home 4-1, Jim Fryatt's goal causing no concern at all.

The next tie, at Maine Road against Spurs, was a tense affair with Tottenham abandoning their usual brand of good football in favour of somewhat violent tactics and they duly paid the penalty when Lee cracked in the only goal of the game in the 64th minute in a move created by Coleman, Bell, Doyle and Summerbee.

Down to Villa Park for the semi-final against Everton and Malcolm Allison gave Dave Connor the role of shadowing Alan Ball, which annoyed the England international so much that he was eventually booked for clattering Connor! Tommy Booth hit home the goal in the dying minutes of the game and City could start to make preparations for a Wembley outing.

The Blues' recent protagonists, Leicester City had also reached the final with a side that featured a young Peter Shilton in goal. Both sides had early chances but it was Manchester City who made the most of one of theirs. After 23 minutes, Summerbee crossed the ball back from the bye-line and Young ran on to it to hammer an unstoppable drive past Shilton. Allan Clarke was Leicester's most dangerous player but Young's goal was enough to win the day. The Foxes also had to suffer relegation to the Second Division, the same fate as City in 1926 after their Wembley outing.

Further FA Cup success became elusive, although other silverware began to fill the Maine Road shelves. In 1969-70 City won both the European Cup-Winners Cup and the League Cup. The next season to note is that of 1980-81. By this time, John Bond was the latest in the Maine Road hot seat as manager and, while he pulled the team out of a steep decline with his popular signings of Bobby McDonald and Tommy Hutchison from Coventry City and Gerry Gow from Bristol City, he could not use these players in City's fine League Cup run as they were all cup-tied. They were eligible for the FA Cup, though, and they all played a significant part in enabling the Blues to arrive yet again at the portals of Wembley.

The third round brought Malcolm Allison's Crystal Palace to Moss Side and, typically, he milked the occasion, waving to the fans who somewhat quickly forgot that he had sold off some gifted and popular players and replaced them with expensive ones with less talent. Allison was left stunned at 4.45pm when the final whistle blew and City had won 4-0 with goals from Kevin Reeves (2, 1 penalty), Paul Power and Phil Boyer. He just could not believe the difference in quality between his side and the Blues.

One of Bond's former clubs, Norwich City, were the next visitors to the Academy, containing in their ranks Joe Royle, David Paul Bennett – an ex-City junior – and Bond's son, Kevin. The Blues went to town in this one, galloping home 6-0 with goals from Power, Reeves, Gow, Steve MacKenzie, David Alan Bennett and McDonald. At the end of the game, Bond senior was so concerned at the disappointment of his son that he leapt out of the Directors' Box to console him … and injured his back!

The fifth round draw saw Tommy Booth score the only goal from a corner at Peterborough United in a game that the home side contested fiercely. The reward was a plum tie against Everton, a match eagerly looked forward to by both sets of fans. The Everton line-up read something like a City one as they had Steve McMahon, Asa Hartford, Imre Varadi and John Gidman playing for them.

Peter Eastoe gave the home side the lead after 43 minutes but, within two minutes, City was level thanks to Gerry Gow, who cleverly flighted a ball into the far corner of the net. Tommy Caton was reckoned by the referee to have committed a heinous crime on Varadi and Trevor Ross scored from the spot, but the day was saved by Paul Power. With six minutes left, Power lobbed the ball over the Everton keeper, Jim McDonough, amid frantic joy from the Manchester contingent and, when Kevin Ratcliffe was sent off a minute later for butting Hutchison, that was the end of Everton's chances.

The replay at Maine Road saw a goalless first half but, after the break, McDonald struck twice, both goals made by Hutchison, and Power hammered the final nail into the Goodison coffin. Eastoe scored a meaningless consolation goal for Everton.

Older City fans were well acquainted with the route to Villa Park. This time, the Blues faced Ipswich Town, an entertaining side who could be hard to overcome. It proved to be exactly that and, at the end of full-time, the score remained goalless although both sides had created reasonable chances. In extra-time, it was once again Paul Power who took the starring role. After 101 minutes of the tie, MacKenzie took a short free-kick and Paul curved the ball with his left foot into the net beyond the reaches of goalkeeper (later-Blue) Paul Cooper.

The Cup Final against Tottenham on 9th May was the Centenary Final. Sadly, that auspicious day for English football was to end in a draw with the replay the following Thursday a major disappointment to City fans.

In the Final, both teams produced some excellent football at times and, after making most of the early, the Blues took the lead after 30 minutes when Hutchison deftly headed home past Aleksic. The Blues' euphoria vanished in the second half when Hutchison got

The 1969 Cup winners.

in the way of a Glenn Hoddle free-kick which was going safely away from the goal, diverting it past the despairing Joe Corrigan.

The Blues fell behind in the replay after seven minutes when Corrigan stopped a shot from Steve Archibald, the ball then running to Ricki Villa who found the net. MacKenzie equalised three minutes later with a 20-yard volley fit to win any final and the Blues went in front through a Reeves penalty after 52 minutes after Bennett had been fouled.

Garth Crooks pulled Spurs onto level terms after 72 minutes, then Villa broke all sky-blue hearts by hitting in the winner, weaving through a City defence that seemed intent on admiring him rather than tackling him. Substitute Dennis Tueart almost grabbed an equaliser but his effort went safely past the post. It was an evening full of sadness for City fans and they were left with an empty feeling of what might have been.

Apart from reaching the sixth round twice, during the 1987-88 season and in 1992-93, losing respectively to Liverpool and Tottenham Hotspur, City's recent Cup form has been disappointing. Hopefully, it won't be too long before the coaches, cars and trains once more descend on Wembley. The loyal City supporters deserve a day out for that special occasion.

The Road to Wembley

The Revie Plan

Bert Trautmann in action.

After Hungary's famous victory over England, it was self-evident that lessons needed to be learnt. The deep-seated insularity of the English game, however, was not easily changed. Les McDowall had a fascination with tactics and was, at that time, one of a small minority of managers in the English league prepared to rethink the way the game was being played. In Don Revie, he found a potent ally.

Revie had signed for the club in 1951 but was continually struggling to find his true position. Too often, he was played upfield, where his lack of pace exposed him. Once the opportunity to play a deeper role arose, his form immediately improved to the extent that he was picked to play for the Football League against the League of Ireland and, by 1954, for England 'B'. McDowall, inspired by the Hungarians, decided to use Don Revie as a deep-lying centre-forward linked-up with Ken Barnes as an attacking wing-half to feed balls through to him. This put pressure on the City defence to cover for Barnes but, with Bert Trautmann's ability at throwing the ball out from a defensive position, the side gained an immediate advantage.

Ken Barnes recalls the new system. 'Les McDowall liked to experiment with different tactical formations, the most famous became known as the Revie Plan. Originally, I played to this system in the reserves with Johnny Williamson; we didn't lose for 30-odd games. The first team tried it at the start of the 1954/55 season at Preston and lost 5-0. However, we persevered and it brought us a lot of success. What confused defences was that they were used to a big centre forward like Nat Lofthouse or Trevor Ford staying up; it was a real battle. The inside forwards and wingers would get the ball into the box for someone to go 'bang'. Against us, all of a sudden, the centre-half had nobody to mark. Our centre-forward, Don Revie, would play a bit deeper and come at them – not be with them all the time. We played the ball in the middle of the park and started linking up. Don, me at wing half, our inside forwards and wingers would alternate, we had a different pattern and it caused problems. When I was running towards our box and saw the ball coming over, I knew Bert would gather the ball and throw it forward quickly because he was great with crosses, so I'd turn the other way to attack. I loved the system. Bert would come out 'here – have it' and I'd be on my way linking up. Going forward with the attack was a piece of cake as far as I was concerned.'

Once the players had become accustomed to the system, the team began to tear apart the opposition. An exhilarating six months of success propelled City up the League and into the semi-final of the FA Cup against Sunderland. Suddenly, two major injuries shook the team's confidence. Johnny Hart, an integral player in the Plan, broke his leg during a League match against Huddersfield Town a week before the semi-final and, during the semi-final, winger Roy Clarke was stretchered off with a bad knee injury.

The team's final League matches showed the stress of competing for two trophies at the same time, a fear that haunted Revie during his years as manager of Leeds United. The wheels had come off the bus and the style that had carried them so confidently through

the season finally deserted them against Newcastle at Wembley.

Don Revie in action.

The Revie Plan, however, had proved it could work. For Don Revie, the season may have ended disappointingly but he had the consolation of being elected Footballer of the Year and winning the first of six international caps.

With so much to look forward to, it was a strange domestic dispute that opened the 1955-56 season. Revie missed pre-season training to take his first family holiday in six years, claiming he had informed the club and had been given permission by the club trainer. McDowall, when he became aware of the arrangement, ordered Revie to commute from his Blackpool holiday every day for training. Revie refused and was suspended for two weeks.

It was said that McDowall never forgave Revie and pushed the player to the margins of the team, first playing him in the reserves whilst the first team struggled and, in all, playing him in fewer that half of that year's League games. Revie, too, was becoming increasingly frustrated by both the manager's attitude and the team's inconsistency and, after the highlight of Wembley, was transferred to Sunderland in November. For City, his loss was significant with a slump to 18th place in the League and exit to Newcastle in the third round of the Cup.

Killer Smog

Although City were desperate to improve on the previous year's failure, their form had hardly been encouraging. Without Revie playing an active role, their confidence was often shakey and Blackpool were certainly not an easy club to start a Cup run against. Roy Paul showed his fighting spirit: 'All cup games are tough and we don't expect this one to be any different from the rest. No one is underestimating the opposition but there is a general feeling of confidence about the result. We had to fight hard to reach Wembley last year and are fully prepared to do even more this year.' Manager Les McDowall was more inclined to rely on Lady Luck: 'We shall go all out from the first whistle and our supporters can depend on the boys giving everything they've got. Having had the good fortune to get a home tie we hope to take advantage of that luck. Everything has been done that could have been done in training, now it must be left to fate whether we get the breaks.' Even less optimistic was soccer writer and broadcaster, Kenneth Wolstenholme who believed City had no chance of winning the FA Cup in 1956 because of his system of picking eight teams for the competition. This took into account past FA Cup history, ruled out the previous season's semi-finalists and the previous season's promoted clubs to Division One. Also, because the League and Cup 'double' had little chance of being achieved, he dismissed teams going for the title. Finally as the First Division elite traditionally won the FA Cup, his tips were Arsenal, Bolton, Chelsea, Everton, Portsmouth, Preston, West Brom and Wolves. Hardly inspiring punditry when none of the eight teams selected managed to make the semi-finals.

The main headline for the Friday Manchester Evening News was 'Killer Smog is Back'. Seven weeks earlier, smog had enveloped the country, killing at least 40 in Manchester alone. This time, the fog had moved up from the South and Midlands and had already brought chaos to road, rail and air traffic. The Cup tie was in doubt and that explained a relatively low attendance of 32,577 on the Saturday. Many supporters had already decided that the match would be postponed and, as it was, the match was almost farcical. The teams came on to the Maine Road pitch to find a heavy mist enveloped the ground, creating doubts about the game surviving the 90 minutes. However, in the immediate period before the kick-off, visibility had improved and the referee quite rightly ordered battle to commence. Ernie Taylor and Stan Matthews had both been pronounced fit and City was fielding an unchanged side for the seventh successive game.

Almost immediately, the huge crowd were stunned into amazed disbelief as Ernie Taylor, after only 30 seconds, had put the visitors in front. Taylor had 'ghosted' in out of the mist on to a through ball from Jack Mudie, to slip the ball past an amazed and still cold Trautmann.

The teams left the field at half time with Blackpool still in the lead and the second half began with the mist continuing to descend. In deteriorating light, Joe Hayes managed to equalise only for the referee to abandon the match after 56 minutes.

The replay was fixed for the following Wednesday, but an earlier kick-off time of 2.15 was sensibly arranged, to avoid a re-run of Saturdays problems. One advantage of Saturday's cancellation was that both teams now knew who their next opponent was, if they were to win through to the next round. A clash with Third Division Southend was an inviting prospect, particularly for City who still had ground advantage against Blackpool.

Although the weather on the Wednesday had improved somewhat, the conditions were little better that the first tie and many supporters were of the opinion that the game should not be played. The programme for the day exonerated referee Harry Webb from Saturday's fiasco although the editor did suggest that it might be more equitable in future if the decision to postpone or abandon a game was delegated to a panel of three.

As the game progressed, City gradually gained control, eventually scoring through Bob Johnstone just before half-time. Seconds later, Bill Perry equalised for Blackpool and the teams trooped into their dressing-rooms all square.

As the game continued in atrocious conditions, the referee was becoming increasingly concerned with his inability to see the line markings. Fortunately, Jack Dyson managed to score after 53 minutes and the Blues held out for a decisive result, much to the relief of the referee and home supporters.

A small footnote about the third round was that City broke their ground receipts for a Cup match – although technically two gates had been recorded.

Sand and Cockleshell Heroes

Fourth Round

25 January 1956

Roots Hall

Attendance 29,500

Receipts £5,572

Manchester City 1

Hayes

Trautmann

Leivers

Little

Barnes

Ewing

Paul

Spurdle

Hayes

Johnstone

Dyson

Clarke

Southend United 0

Threadgold

Williamson

Howe

Duthie

Stirling

Lawler

Lockheart

McGrory

Hollis

Baron

McGuigan

The weather once again made the headlines. Torrential rain had been lashing the Essex coast for days and there were serious doubts expressed as to the state of the pitch. Manchester Evening News reporter, Eric Thornton, arrived at the ground as workmen were digging up the turf. The ordinary drains were not working efficiently enough and the chairman, a farmer, had ordered a zig-zag trench to be cut across the pitch, the drains opened and tons of cockle shells poured into them before the soil was relaid. Thornton's story was soon picked up and some of the national press even considered the state of the ground might give Southend a shock win.

Certainly, the City players were far from impressed when they arrived for the game. Ken Barnes recollects: 'The Southend game was played on a new ground, just opened. Before the game some of the lads went onto the pitch to have a look. They said you'll never be able to pass the ball on this pitch, and you couldn't. It was abominable; to try and play the game was dreadful. When you walked out your feet sank about four inches. How we played I don't know, it was horrendous and a real slog.'

Once again, the referee considered that the game was playable and for a time, the press predictions of a giant-killing did not seem far-fetched as Southend, used to the quagmire of a pitch, attacked with ferocity. The 25,000 Southend supporters, struggling to stay upright on the slippery terraces, were relishing the First Division side's discomfort

as City struggled to come to terms with the conditions and it was left to one man to keep the Third Division side at bay. As Roy Paul commented afterwards: 'The pitch was dreadful to play on and most of the lads came off with skinned knees caused by sand and shells. One man got us through that match – Bert Trautmann.'

With Southend committed to attack, City countered and Joe Hayes broke away to score after 25 minutes. From then on, it was simply a matter of closing down the Southend attack. An appeal from Southend for a penalty was denied in a game few of the City players could recall with any affection. Roy Clarke summarised the match: 'The pitch had masses of sand all over it to help drain the water but it made play impossible; there were cockleshells everywhere. Bert played one of his best games and made one of his finest saves ever; I can still see it now. The ball was heading in like a rocket; he was going one way, then had to switch but he just managed to get a touch to it. If that had gone in we could easily have lost. At the other end, Johnny Hart played a ball in to me; it went 'plop'. All I had to do was tap it in but the wind blew the ball behind me and I missed completely. The papers next day called us the 'Sand and Cockleshell Heroes'. We did really well to win that day.'

Opposite Training was repetitious and boring – usually involving countless laps around the Maine Road pitch.

Through the wind and rain ... and snow and ice!

Fifth Round

18 February 1956

Maine Road

Attendance 70,640

Receipts £9,453

Manchester City 0

Trautmann

Leivers

Little

Barnes

Ewing

Paul

Spurdle

Hayes

Revie

Dyson

Johnstone

Liverpool 0

Underwood

Molyneux

Moran

Saunders

Hughes

Twentyman

Payne

Arnell

Liddell

Evans

A'Court

he Fifth Round draw was again kind to the Blues, with another home tie against lower division opposition but, for the third tie running, weather made the headlines. Heavy snow had fallen and once again, the match was in doubt. Also in doubt was the fitness of Roy Clarke, giving Les McDowall the opportunity to accommodate the undoubtedly talented Revie, bring back Bill Spurdle on the right wing and move the versatile Bob Johnstone over to left wing.

Inches of snow had been cleared from the field and both teams came out early to get a feel of the conditions and the very treacherous surface. The snow had been stacked around the perimeter wall and both penalty areas liberally sanded, before the kick-off

Both teams soon found the icy surface difficult and the unyielding surface was more conducive to skating than football. An incredible crowd of over 70,000 had turned out in expectation of a classic cup-tie between a struggling First Division side and a confident Second Division one but the quality of the game was hardly fitting on a day when the slippery pitch made constructive football almost impossible. The final score of 0-0 had been predictable for a long time, with both sides happy to escape any serious injuries. The prospect of a replay at Anfield in front of their passionate fans was more appealing to Liverpool than City. An added incentive for the Merseysiders was the Sixth Round draw which had drawn the winners of the tie against Everton.

The prospect of a Liverpool 'derby' encouraged in-form Billy Liddell to wax lyrically about his team's chance: 'I know a game is never won until it is lost, yet the more I think of having another crack at City tomorrow the more confident I am that this time we'll put the issue beyond doubt. True, City missed several chances in the Maine Road game – but isn't that Cup football all over? In view of the conditions underfoot, I thought it a very good game and particularly remembering we had a goal disallowed for offside. I don't think we were flattered by finishing level. Our defence came out with flying colours and, taken all round, I can't think of any Liverpool weak links.

At the moment, the Anfield pitch is bone-hard – and that's another reason I fancy our chances of making that Sixth Round date. I have a suspicion that City are more apt to be put off their stroke on these hard surfaces and I am looking forward to quicker tackling upsetting their ideas in front of goal.'

Eric Thornton's match report in the Manchester Evening News tried to raise spirits after the disappointment of losing home advantage. 'Everybody seems to have written off Manchester City's experimental Cup line-up because it failed against Liverpool. They want wholesale changes for Wednesday's replay at Anfield. I am in favour of at least one switch while remembering two points which seem to have been forgotten – the conditions and Joe Hayes. I know it is the same for both sides but frozen conditions were right against the anticipated success of the new attack ... there must be closer analysis and that reveals the big fault – at centre-forward. There Don Revie was a mere shadow of the man who was in such great form last season. He wandered in and out of the game without lending much support to anyone.'

With Don Revie effectively blamed for the failure of the Blues to capitalise on the opportunities they had created, Thornton's analysis became more upbeat: 'The odds were in City's favour before the start. At half time they had narrowed. Today the odds will have lengthened though they will, in my opinion, win through at the second attempt.

Why? Because it is impossible to believe any of the forwards can again miss such grand scoring opportunities. Over the years they have some happy recollections of Anfield. Their next visit should be one to add to the list, especially if the long pass is used more frequently and first time shooting becomes popular again. They must stop fiddling in the goalmouth. They must stop 'holding' the ball too long. And they must keep it low when aiming at the target.'

With these words of wisdom ringing in their ears, it was off to Anfield to face the might of the Kop.

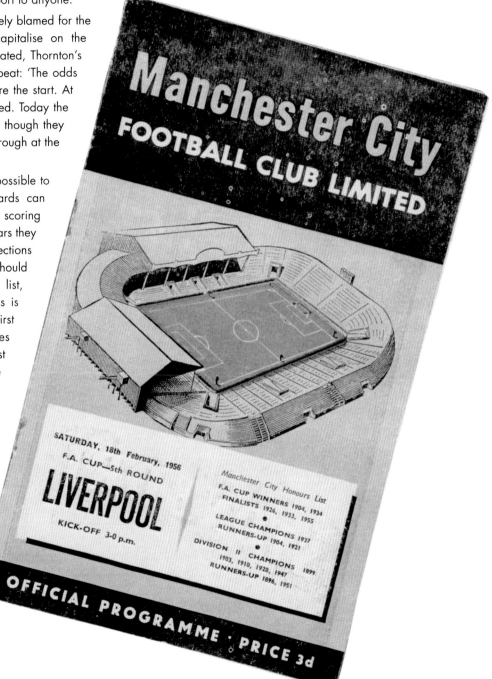

Last minute drama at Anfield

Fifth Round Replay

Wednesday 22 February
Anfield
Attendance 57,520
Receipts £6,978

Manchester City 2
Dyson, Hayes

Trautmann
Leivers
Little
Barnes
Ewing
Paul
Spurdle
Hayes
Revie
Dyson
Johnstone

Liverpool 1
Arnell

Underwood
Molyneux
Moran
Saunders
Hughes
Twentyman
Payne
Arnell
Liddell
Evans
A'Court

Don Revie's return to the side had been disappointing. To be fair, no one had shone in the first tie but the transfer-listed Revie had not shone or scored in his run of three matches in place of the injured Roy Clarke. The return to fitness of Roy Clarke allowed McDowall to move Johnstone inside with Clarke playing in his familiar left wing role.

City supporters flooded Liverpool city centre, chanting, clattering rattles and ringing bells. Snow was swirling outside Anfield with such ferocity that ground officials took pity on the thousands who had arrived up to four hours early and, at midday, opened the gates so that the supporters could shelter in the stands. Another huge crowd of 57,528 turned out on another miserable afternoon although the pitch was at least playable.

The game started almost sensationally when Bert Trautmann committed one of his rare errors. Coming from his line to collect a back pass, he only succeeded in pushing into the path of a Liverpool forward, who promptly lobbed it back into the area with Bert stranded miles off his line in no-mans land. Billy Liddell and Bill Leivers went up together with Leivers successful in deflecting the ball onto the crossbar and over for a corner. This led to some considerable Liverpool pressure but City managed to defend successfully up to the interval with high expectations for a great second half.

The second period began with City trying to expose the Liverpool defence with the pace of Roy Clarke on the left wing, but it was Liverpool who opened the scoring through Arnell in the 52nd minute, crashing the ball home from four yards. As Liverpool pressed

forward, City had to consolidate at the back and began to force themselves back into the game. In the 65th minute, the pressure paid off with an equaliser from Jack Dyson following some skillful play from Bob Johnstone who, gathering a ball in midfield, went past two challenges and slipped a beautiful ball out to Bill Spurdle. Spurdle's cross picked out Dyson who, with some skill, chipped it past goalkeeper Underwood.

Liverpool was visibly shaken by this effort and hit back with ferocious attacks but City encouraged by being now back in the game, was equally determined and fully playing its part in what was now a thrilling cup-tie. A draw looked likely again with only a couple of minutes left to play, when Bob Johnstone unlocked the Liverpool defence and slipped a through ball for Joe Hayes to control and crack into the Liverpool net.

Then, with time almost up, Liverpool mounted a ferocious assault on the City goal. The home crowd had worked themselves into a frenzy and, in what proved to be one of those great Cup 'moments', Liddle cracked the ball past Bert Trautmann, only to discover that the final whistle had gone as he struck the ball. The Liverpool players surrounded referee Griffiths to make their protest but to no avail. The goal was disallowed. It was all over and City was through to the Sixth Round.

No. 32

LIVERPOOL
FOOTBALL CLUB
SEASON 1955-56

Directors:
W. J. HARROP, J.P. (Chairman)
T. V. WILLIAMS (Vice-Chairman)
R. L. MARTINDALE, M.B.E., J.P.   T. McCONNELL
G. A. RICHARDS, J.P.   H. CARTWRIGHT
H. ROBSON ROBERTS.   C. J HILL.
S. C. REAKES, J.P.   J. S. McINNES (Secretary)
D. WELSH (Manager)

F.A. CUP—5th ROUND (Replay)

LIVERPOOL v. MANCHESTER CITY
AT ANFIELD
WEDNESDAY, 22nd FEBRUARY, 1956
Kick-off 2-45 p.m.

OFFICIAL   PROGRAMME
PRICE   THREEPENCE

Opposite Jack Dyson challenges for the ball in the snow.

Ken Barnes has clear memories of the game and controversy: 'At Liverpool, the weather was appalling. Even so, we played well that night and deserved the win. The incident fans remember was when the referee blew for time just as Liddell scored what would have been their equaliser. I remember him having possession down the left flank, the crowd was going wild, he hit this ball and it just squeezed in. We were already shaking hands on the half way line!'

Roy Clarke had good reason to believe the result was fair: 'I pulled a muscle before the first game at Maine Road and went to hospital on the Monday to get it right for the replay. I got changed, walked to the theatre with a nurse where the specialist, doctor and our trainer were waiting. They told me to lay flat on the floor where they would stretch my muscle as far as it would go. They pulled my foot towards my neck until it could go no further! I went out against Liverpool and the muscle tweaked within five minutes. Fortunately, it didn't go completely, otherwise I'd have had to go off. In the last minute, Liddell hit this ball from 20 yards and the ball was going in. The referee was standing next to me on the half way line and he goes 'peep', game over. The ball went in and he turned to me; 'It didn't reach the goal when I blew the whistle.' We were relieved!'

After the game Liddell's late strike was the main topic of discussion. Everyone had a viewpoint but most people accepted that either the referee blew his whistle as Liddell made his run, or that he blew his whistle as Liddell shot. Photographic evidence in the Manchester Evening News certainly appeared to support this latter view. In the background of one photograph, the referee can be clearly seen signalling the end of the game as City players jump for joy and two walk off the pitch. Leslie McDowall commented, 'I didn't even see the shot. Once I heard the referee's whistle, I immediately stood up in the stand and walked over to Don Welsh. Then there was a roar and on turning around I noticed Trautmann picking the ball out of the net. That time lag alone surely proves that Liddell's shot was made after the final whistle had gone.' Roy Paul added, 'There should be no doubt about it. Having heard the final whistle, I turned towards the dressing room entrance as Liddell closed in on goal and shot.' As for the referee, he was adamant Liddell scored fifteen seconds after he blew the final whistle.

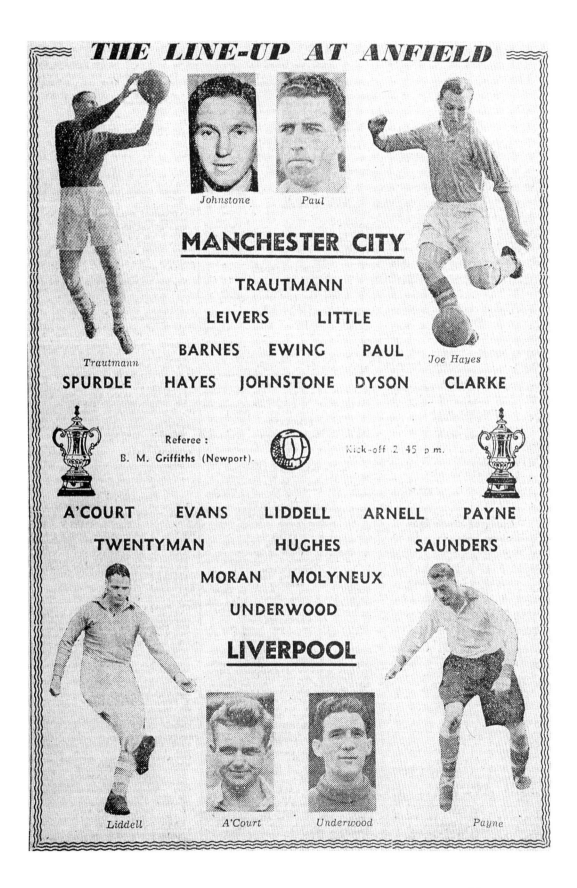

Johnstone   Paul

MANCHESTER CITY

TRAUTMANN

LEIVERS   LITTLE

BARNES   EWING   PAUL

SPURDLE   HAYES   JOHNSTONE   DYSON   CLARKE

Trautmann

Joe Hayes

Referee :
B. M. Griffiths (Newport).

Kick-off 2.45 p.m.

A'COURT   EVANS   LIDDELL   ARNELL   PAYNE

TWENTYMAN   HUGHES   SAUNDERS

MORAN   MOLYNEUX

UNDERWOOD

LIVERPOOL

Liddell   A'Court   Underwood   Payne

Another Scouse Scalp

For Blues fans with long memories, the 1933 Cup Final was not a day to reflect on, with Everton drubbing them 3-0. Fortunately, there was no Dixie Dean facing them this time around. The luck of the draw had given City home advantage for the third time and against their old rivals, they needed all the luck they could get. Cup fever had lifted the home support and another astonishing gate of over 70,000 welcomed both teams on to the field. Late injury checks had cleared Bert Trautmann and Roy Clarke although the 'medical' was somewhat primitive, as Clarke recalls: 'I had a fitness test before the game with Lawrie Farm. He said 'right … laps … sprints … now get your boots on'. I thought: 'Great, I'll be kicking the ball now, I can really test my knee'. He takes me to the touch line puts my hands on the wall and says, 'right … kick the hell out of the wall with the toes of your boots, then we'll know if you're fit!'

Everton won the toss and decided to play with the light wind behind them The game started with both teams playing cautiously and very tight at the back, giving no room to the forwards of either side. Vigorous by play by Dave Ewing and the usual composure and assurance of Trautmann prevented any problems around the home goal but City were getting no change out of the strong Everton defence.

Everton soon began to make the pace and their pressure caused more than a few hearts to miss a beat when a thrilling move down the left flank ended with a perfect header from Eglington. Bert Trautmann made an instinctive save but his clearance was too short, falling at the feet of Wainwright. Bert dived at the forward's feet and managed to smother the ball amidst ringing cheers from Everton's packed supporters. With Everton in control, Trautmann was again called into action when he pushed away a superb Farrell free kick.

Surprisingly, it was City who found themselves in the best scoring position in the 12th minute, when Spurdle found Dyson unmarked in the Everton penalty area. With virtually an open net in front of him, the young forward pulled his shot wide when it looked easier to score.

That opportunity apart, it was Everton who were making the running and another superb shot from Wainwright looked as if it was heading for the corner of the net when Leivers managed to get his foot in first to deflect the ball. Another cunning shot from the lively Wainwright was saved by Trautmann to tumultuous applause from the home support but Bert had little chance in the 27th minute when Brian Harris fashioned a move that left Jimmy Harris ten yards out at an acute angle. Bert managed to get his fingertips to the ball but his sterling efforts could not keep the ball from hitting the back of the net to the accompaniment of one of the largest cheers heard at Maine Road for some time. Everton had taken the lead and City were struggling to contain them.

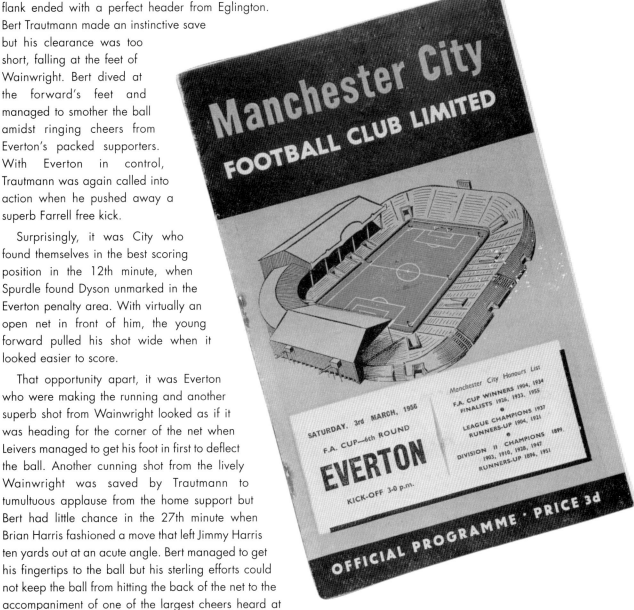

Opposite Medical checks were usually somewhat lacking in sophistication.

Only some great goalkeeping by Bert Trautmann prevented Everton increasing their lead with Harris and Eglington causing the City defence all kinds of problems. Wearing a cap to protect his eyes against the sun, Trautmann had to be at his best to fingertip away another superb shot after Harris and Eglington had bamboozled the City defence.

Half-time could not come quickly enough for hard-pressed City who were perhaps fortunate that only one goal separated the two teams.

Everton came out in the second half intent on putting the game beyond doubt and Leivers, in particular, was having problems with marking Eglington. When he did finally catch up with the elusive winger, his rather inappropriate tackle left the player writhing around on the ground. Referee Bond was less than amused, admonishing Leivers with a stern warning.

Bill Leivers' tackle seemed to mark a turning point in the game, and the incident curtailed Everton adventures down the left flank. The rest of the City players took encouragement and began to approach the game with more confidence. It was now Everton's turn to have problems as City came more into the game. Bob Johnstone and Joe Hayes were beginning to dominate and the whole side had found a new rhythm. Ken Barnes and Roy Paul were now supporting the front men and both Clarke and Spurdle were beginning to find space on the wings.

The finishing touch was still eluding them, Dyson in particular having a nightmare game. City were making all of the running and the Everton players were having difficulty

Previous page Action from the Sixth Round clash with Everton.

Below Johnstone heads home in the 75th minute to win the game for City.

getting back into the game. At last, in the 69th minute, a perfect Roy Paul free kick into the penalty area found Joe Hayes who squeezed between two big Everton defenders and nodded home the equaliser.

The cheers from over 60,000 supporters had hardly died down when the ball was in the back of the net again. This time the referee had no hesitation in disallowing it, having seen Roy Clarke helping the ball into the goal with his hand.

Within minutes, Clarke was in action again, crossing to Bob Johnstone who scored with a glorious header in the 75th minutes. With City now in full control, the last fifteen minutes were now a celebration for the City fans. Roy Paul's promise after the 1955 Final now seemed to be coming good and the Maine Road fans left in high spirits, looking forward to the semi final draw, with a feeling that this was to be their year.

Spurs are 'Robbed'

The semi-final draw paired City with either West Ham or Spurs. Manager Leslie McDowall was upbeat about his sides' prospects. 'We don't mind which team has to play us in the next stage because all the boys feel very confident that this is really going to be their year. It just suits us fine and everybody at the club is very satisfied with this draw.' In the event, it turned out to be Tottenham Hotspur who defeated West Ham 2-1 against expectation. Spurs were old protagonists in the Cup, most recently in 1954, when they had beaten the Blues 1-0 in a third round tie. The Londoners were struggling in the League but had an excellent defence with Norman, Hopkins and the masterly Danny Blanchflower.

Not for the first time in this cup campaign, City started sluggishly. As both sides were competing for control, the Blues had the first scare when Danny Blanchflower crashed a free kick just wide of Trautmann's goal and into the side netting. Spurs was playing attractively with its push and run style, which encouraged great movement and was continually causing problems for the City defence. Luck was with City when Spurs centre forward Smith tucked a ball into the bottom corner of the net, only for it to be disallowed by the referee.

In a scrappy first-half, the best moment for City fans came in the 40th minute as Roy Clarke recalls: 'Bobby Johnstone scored our goal, out-jumping their two fullbacks and

goalkeeper to head home; amazing when you realise he was five feet nothing. Originally, he picked up the ball on the halfway line and, thinking six moves ahead as usual, played it to me before setting off. I've got the ball and I'm going at the full back, who's a long way from me and Bobby shouts 'hold it ... hold on ... hang on to it'. The full back is getting closer and I'm thinking 'come on ... hurry up ... quick'. Then he shouts 'right' and I crossed it, out comes the goalkeeper and two full backs and he scores ... unbelievable ... he out-jumped the lot of them. What impressed me most was that he made the move himself, a wonderful player.'

City came out in the second half determined to keep the initiative and Spurs' keeper Reynolds was far more active than Trautmann. Barnes and Paul now began to control the midfield. Spurs even switched their wingers in an effort to unsettle City at the back and then moved centre half Maurice Norman into the attack. He did get one chance but defenders are not forwards and the chance went begging.

City kept their heads and refused to be panicked. Spurs desperation was obvious when Danny Blanchflower began pushing everybody forward to try and get back in the game. But, by this time, City was well in control with Ken Barnes and Roy Paul in midfield and Trautmann controlling the defensive situation from the back.

As the match was drawing to what seemed an inevitable victory for City, the most talked about incident of the match occurred. In Roy Clarke's words: 'With a few minutes left we were still a goal up and fighting to stay in control when Bert fouled George Robb as he broke through on the edge of our box. He was very fortunate not to be sent off and it could easily have been a penalty. Every team needs a bit of luck in the Cup, when you added this moment to Liddell's last second strike that was ruled out, we really thought this could be our year.'

Bert Trautmann hold his hands up to the professional foul: 'Bobby Johnstone scored a great goal then, towards the end of the game, there was a melee of players on the edge

Opposite The team pulling together for Wembley.

43

The FOOTBALL ASSOCIATION CHALLENGE CUP
No. 3545
SEMI-FINAL
AT VILLA PARK, BIRMINGHAM.
Saturday, March 17th, 1956.
Kick-off 3·0 p.m.
RESERVED SEAT £1/5/0 Including Tax
Row E
Seat No. 127
ENTRANCE DOOR
WITTON LANE F
THIS PORTION TO BE RETAINED
Secretary,
Aston Villa F.C. Ltd.

of our penalty box, I dived in. it was just one of those things. During a game you do lots of things instinctively, you have at times less than a second to decide what to do. You certainly don't have time to always plan things. Yes, I fouled him but it happens in lots of games. I had to, otherwise it would probably have been a goal and we may not have gone to Wembley. A few days later we went to London for a league match with Spurs. Before the game, we went to the local picture-house and, to my amazement, the incident was on the Movietone news. The reporter said: 'Now watch German goalkeeper Bert Trautmann fouling George Robb by holding his legs', I couldn't believe it, with all the news stories available they included this incident.'

The Spurs' fans were incensed, especially with newspapers featuring photographs of Bert holding Robb's leg. When City faced Spurs the following Saturday in an away League match, Bert faced some of the worst abuse since his first matches for the Blues. City lost the match but Bert played courageously and gained considerable respect from the majority of the crowd.

The threatening letters and abuse directed at the goalkeeper were soon forgotten when Bert was awarded the coveted Player of the Year by the Football Writers' Association. Not only was he the second City player in succession to win, after Don Revie in 1955, but, more importantly, the first foreign player and first goalkeeper.

Personally, it had been a great year for Bert but one great challenge remained, a chance to win a major trophy with the club he loved. Local rivals Manchester United had already won the League and now it fell to City to make it a Manchester double.

Wembley now beckoned but in the Evening News, Eric Thornton had a few words of caution. Under a headline 'Form Not Good Enough For Final', Thornton took the team to task: 'I hope Manchester City players heed the gypsy's warnings. They were told at the turn of the year that they'd get to the Final again, but have a fright just before reaching Wembley from a lack of aggressiveness. That was exactly what happened at Villa Park. The forwards were too often out of touch, hesitant and easily dispossessed. If they had only revealed their form of recent weeks, the game would have been 'in the bag' for them long before the end.

Bobby Johnstone was as lively as ever. He never seems to tire or lose his efficiency, though he sometimes found the going hard against constant shadowing by Danny Blanchflower. Roy Clarke was generally cool and confident, especially with those long centres which had the Spurs defence scrambling. But the other forwards were patchy.

It was a different story in defence where, for once, Bert Trautmann wasn't as busy as usual. I rate Roy Little's performance very high and must commend Bill Leivers on a fight back to better form in the second half. But chief credit goes to the halves. First of all to Roy Paul for his great captaincy, drive and planning. Then to Ken Barnes for his mobility and the clever manner in which he constantly slipped up among the forwards. And finally to David Ewing for wholehearted endeavour.

I think it was fine team spirit that got them through. But they'll need to be in better form as an attacking machine when they come up against Birmingham City in the Final.'

Previous page Action from the Semi Final against Spurs.

Opposite Building up team spirit before Wembley.

One Last Push!

FA Cup Final
Wembley Stadium
5 May 1956
Attendance 100,000

Manchester City 3
Hayes, Dyson, Johnstone

Trautmann
Leivers
Little
Barnes
Ewing
Paul
Johnstone
Hayes
Revie
Dyson
Clarke

Birmingham City 1
Kinsey

Merrick
Hall
Green
Newman
Smith
Boyd
Astall
Kinsey
Brown
Murphy
Govan

With a place at Wembley booked, the one major hurdle facing supporters was to get hold of a ticket. Every year, the controversy of distribution raised its head. This year was no different for City supporters alone could have filled the famous stadium. The Manchester Evening News was appalled with the ticket allocation. They told fans that their chances of getting a ticket would be '2-1 against', stating the system was 'wrong and out of date'. They commented: 'Give to the genuine football followers, the men and women who keep the clubs alive and whose team fights through to Wembley, a better deal. Give the two finalists a better allocation. With an average gate of over 37,000, City fans were disappointed to learn that the club's allocation would be half of the finalists allocation of 30,000 with prices at 50s, 25s, 15s, 10s 6d, and 3s 6d. Many fans enquired where the other tickets went; the Manchester Evening News supplied the information, FA 4,640 Finalists 30,000 County Associations 40,640 League Clubs 20,090, FA Members 2,550 FA Council and Stadium Authorities 2,080.

Ticket touts were not as evident as usual; probably due to the blackmarket ticket inquiry following the previous seasons Cup Final. However, 3s 6d tickets were selling for £3 and 10s 6d ones were changing hands for between £6 and £7 each. In Manchester city centre, one tout commented, 'All I've got available at the moment are the dearer ones. I was cleaned out of the 3s 6d ones yesterday; they fetched upwards of £4 a time. I have seventeen at the moment, some are 15s tickets which I'll let go for £8 10s each, and some are 25s ... they'll be £10 10s each.' In Birmingham one coach party of sixty-four paid £320 so they could all get in.

For the players, the build-up started as with the previous year, with the team travelling to Eastbourne a week before the match to their headquarters at the Queens Hotel. Don Revie travelled but was not expected to play. In an article in the Evening News he had penned some thoughts about Cup training which must have been hard for the transfer-listed and out of favour player.

Under the headline 'Pep Training No Guarantee for Cup Success', Revie wrote: 'Football fans, most of whom take their holidays in mid-summer, are apt to be sarcastic about pampered footballers going away for special training at spa towns or the seaside. How worthwhile they ask is this toning up in brine baths. Frankly my opinion is that special Cup training does no good at all. In my opinion, it is more important to take the lads away for a breather for league matches rather than key Cup matches ... we at Manchester City found that before last year's Cup Final, the days at Eastbourne dragged. The dangers of taking players away for special training are:

1) they have too much time on their hands

2) they train hard and then tend to over-eat and spend too much time relaxing in armchairs or playing cards.

3) change of food and air can, in fact, upset some highly trained players.'

However, Revie concluded that, if he were manager with a side threatened with relegation or promotion, or before the crucial Easter period when most League issues are decided, he would take his players away for a break to refresh them.

With three days to go, all rail and air accommodation to London had been booked, although some coach seats were available. For fans without tickets, there was a growing resignation that they would have to stay behind and watch the Final on television. Eighty six year old Mrs H Hall of Grimsby was one of the lucky ones. She was told by 'Have a Go' host Wilfred Pickles that he would try to get her a ticket. But when the BBC replied that they could not get her any, listeners contacted FA Chairman Arthur Drewery, also from Grimsby, with the result that two tickets were forthcoming for Mrs Hall and her grandson.

In the City camp, injuries were the major issue with Bill Leivers and Bobby Johnstone particular worries. As the week progressed, the fitness of both players improved and it was a shock when right winger Bill Spurdle developed a serious attack of boils. Les McDowall had to face a possible tactical rethink and the option of playing Revie in his favourite deep role. Most of the players favoured Revie but playing alongside Johnstone not instead of him, to give a greater attacking option. When Spurdle was finally ruled out, McDowall made his choice and the two players were in the team.

Cup Final Saturday was dry and mild. The huge exodus from Manchester was underway, although many had left the day before, to make a weekend out of the event and Trafalgar Square, in particular, was a meeting point for fans of both clubs. With rattles clacking and bells ringing, they filled the streets of London with good-hearted banter and singing.

Towards midday, the mass of supporters headed off towards Wembley to claim their places and to enjoy the tradition of community singing and brass band displays. Birmingham City had surprisingly been installed as favourites but Blues fans were confident that their club's name had been on the Cup from the start of the competition.

The players may have been getting their attack of pre-match nerves but the crowd were being entertained by the band of the Royal Marines followed by community singing led by the ever–present Arthur Caiger. The solemn finale of 'Abide With Me' was the cue for the crowd to concentrate its emotions before the final formalities of the National Anthem and royal presentation were observed.

Roy Paul led his team out of the tunnel to tumultuous applause. As both teams normal colours were blue, both sides had to change, City into their alternative claret and blue stripes and Birmingham into white shirts and blue shorts. Paul was fully charged up and gave his team-mates and the opposition, no doubt as to his intention to win. He had already expressed his opinion to the press: 'This present City team is one that seems to thrive on a fight, and I feel certain that this time we shall have the proper reward to show

at the end of it. All our boys have by now become accustomed to playing before big crowds, so there should not be much fear about Wembley jitters.'

Roy Clarke remembers feeling the tension: Before the game we were more relaxed than the previous year because we knew what to expect, we really thought we could beat Birmingham. They didn't have any really classy footballers like us and our movement on the pitch was smooth, which suited Wembley. I loved playing at Wembley; it was magnificent, if you kicked the ball from the right half position to me on the left wing it rolled along the pitch perfectly, I could turn away shut my eyes and stop the ball; that's how perfect the surface was.

Before the game, everyone prepares differently. Some players go to the toilets a million times, others can't stop talking, others go white … completely silent. Jack Dyson changed next to me and was so nervous he put my boots on! During the team talk, McDowall went over our roles one more time, even though we all knew them. He also reminded us of the previous year when we let in an early goal and told us not to 'carry the ball too much', because the pitch could be energy sapping. When you received the

ball your natural inclination was to run a mile because the ground was so perfect. He emphasised 'tire the ball out … not yourselves'. Then it was time to go, when we left the dressing room I knew we weren't going to go back as losers. We were ready!

Waiting in the tunnel was the worst part; I was petrified. As usual I was behind Roy and he was really fired up, I can still see him shaking his fist to encourage us, I think it unnerved the Birmingham players! The noise was incredible as we walked out. I remember the presentations before the game because the guests of honour certainly do their homework. The Duke of Edinburgh came down the line and chatted with Bert; they had a bit of a giggle. I'm next to Trauty, he shakes my hand … 'how's your leg?', obviously someone had told him I'd missed out the previous year; I was impressed.

The nerves completely went when the match started. Even though you knew you were playing at Wembley, you had to concentrate as if it was just another match. Of course, being on the wing, you'd cop the lot whether it was from fans, the manager, trainer, reserves, they'd all be telling you how to play. However, at Wembley, you can only hear shouting, not who they're shouting for, so I just told myself they were shouting for me and took it as encouragement.'

In some respects, I was fortunate to be playing because I was still having trouble with my knee but the manager decided to risk it. During the game I remember flicking my cartilage back in because it slipped out, really I shouldn't have played but the gamble was worth it.'

Joe Hayes' sensational opening goal after two and a half minutes.

Ken Barnes, also remembers feeling the tension, particularly because of his

Birmingham background: 'Against Birmingham, we were allowed to buy around 100 tickets. Being a Brummie, I had this relation and that relation, so the whole lot quickly went; it cost me a fortune!'

At Wembley, it's hard to savour the atmosphere because so much is going on. When you arrive, you can't wait to get on with the game, you just think 'I hope I do all right today.' They used to say the pitch affected your legs ... that it was energy sapping; but I never believed that. To me it was simply the occasion that effected you.

Losing in '55 made us really determined. Okay, we were at Wembley again but we didn't want to lose this time. Before the game, McDowall got a bit carried away, he said to me 'keep a tight reign on Murphy, he's a poacher ... their goal scorer'. I said, 'keep a tight reign? I've got to look up and do a bit of running and support the attackers.' But he insisted, 'keep a tight reign on him!' I wasn't happy, 'it's all very well you saying that but I can't be in two places at once'. Anyway I played as instructed but at the interval, Don wasn't happy with me, 'Where've you been?' I said, 'You heard him in the dressing room before we came out, what do you want me to do? Stay with him ... that's easy ... but what about playing and linking up'. Don roared, 'Come on ... play!'

The match kicked off to the usual deafening roar from the crowd and Manchester immediately played their Revie Plan to devastating effect. Revie picked up the ball, passed to Clarke and ran fifty yards for the return pass on the left of the penalty area, and flicked the ball to Joe Hayes who blasted his shot past Merrick. Three minutes had passed and City were in the lead.

Don Revie runs to congratulate Jack Dyson on scoring City's second goal.

To Roy Clarke, the goal was a total vindication of their system: 'I remember our first goal because Bill Leivers had been suffering with an ankle injury and couldn't kick a long ball, so when he received the ball from Bert, he played it short to Ken; linking up as usual. Ken passed it to Don who then played it across to me shouting 'hang on', because he wanted to go past me. Their full back was coming over and I thought 'bloody hell', cause he's a big lad, Don went past and I played the ball just inside – a diagonal to him. He ran over it, flicked it between his legs and on to Joe Hayes who knocked it in the far corner. I've always thought that goal was a shining example of the Revie Plan.'

The Birmingham players were stunned and it took twenty minutes before they worked themselves back into the match and brought the first real save from Trautmann who parried the shot away for a corner. An even more dangerous move after thirty minutes saw Kinsey strike a superb shot which hit the post before finding the back of the net.

The teams trooped into their respective dressing-rooms with honours equal. Don Revie recalled Les McDowall's half-time talk: 'The manager told us: 'Bring the ball down and use it. Don't panic, no big kicking. At Wembley pure football, style and skill will always pay dividends.' Even at half time he told us, 'One last push lads. Just keep playing the same way and the goals will come.''

As play resumed after the interval, City began to play the kind of football that they were capable of yet so often had failed to deliver. The match was no classic but this was partly due to City's control, closing Birmingham down and giving them little space to develop any meaningful moves. Revie was having a masterful game and confidence was flowing through the side.

Johnstone wraps it up for City.

The reward for their pressure did not take long to come. On 57 minutes, Dyson picked on a through ball from Johnstone and pushed it passed the hapless Merrick. Birmingham rallied and launched their own attack, only for Trautmann to pick up the ball and launch an immediate counter-attack. The ball found Revie who spotted Dyson and Johnstone unmarked. As the Birmingham players rushed back to defend their goal, Dyson pushed a ball through for Johnstone to make the score 3-1.

At this stage Ken Barnes was certain of victory: 'Birmingham came into it a bit more in the second half but really we should have won by four or five at the finish, we had some great chances. However when you're 3-1 up with a quarter of an hour to go, you say to yourself, 'we're okay, keep it tight.''

But with the pressure off, City lost the sense of urgency, allowing Birmingham back into the game. In a move which has become one of the great moments of Cup history, Peter Murphy, the Birmingham inside-left, chased a ball into the penalty area clear of the City defence. Bert Trautmann instinctively dived at his feet and cleared the ball only to make sickening contact with Murphy's knee.

Immediately, referee Bond stopped the game and trainer Laurie Barnett ran onto the pitch. Bert was lying semi-conscious on the ground and, as he slowly got to his feet, the implication of his injury hit the City players. Their goalkeeper was clearly unfit to carry on, he was unsteady on his feet and in considerable pain. Thoughts of who might take his place were brushed aside by the brave keeper. Since substitutes were not allowed, his only option was to play on.

The moment of drama as Bert Trautmann lies injured in his goalmouth.

Birmingham were obviously greatly encouraged by the situation now facing them and,

with just over 15 minutes, they still had time to secure a result. Within minutes another attack brought Trautmann rushing out to dive at Brown's feet. City's defence now had only one objective, to kick the ball as far out of their half as possible.

Birmingham had not finished and, as Brown attacked again, Ewing collided with his own keeper, bringing Trautmann down on the ground again. Time was fast running out and when the full-time whistle blew, the Blues had finally fulfilled Roy Paul's prophesy – the Cup was theirs at last.

For Bert Trautmann, the hero of the day, most of the proceedings were just a haze. Others, including Roy Clarke, had a more vivid recall:'In the second half we got on top and should have scored a few more. We were knocking the ball about and they tired; experience told in the end. At the final whistle, I just grabbed the nearest player to me before commiserating with our opponents. When we went up the steps to the Royal Box to receive the Cup, I followed Roy Paul. The Queen handed him the Cup and his medal, then he showed it to our supporters; the noise was incredible. I remember us all jumping around during the lap of honour before going back to the dressing room; the feeling of relief was immense. We put champagne in the Cup and everyone who could get in came in, it was a brilliant atmosphere.'

After the dressing-room celebrations, it was off to the Cafe Royal for the traditional celebration dinner with their wives. Bert was looking increasingly uncomfortable, the pain was actually getting worse and his head was tilted at an angle. Amazingly, no medical examination had taken place, as Bert recalls: 'Of course the '56 Final was a terrific highlight in my career. Wembley is known throughout the world so to play there and win was fantastic. After the Final, no doctor examined my neck, it was as if I had toothache. On the Sunday morning, I went to St George's Hospital in Kensington and the junior doctors were on. I had an X-ray and they said I'd ricked my neck. We went back

Roy Paul receives the Cup from HM The Queen.

to Manchester for the civic reception; the crowds were amazing. I wasn't feeling good though and someone took me inside. Frank Swift came over and slapped me on the shoulder to congratulate me, it's amazing I didn't pass out.'

For the other players, there was now time to savour their achievement although the rewards were spiritual rather than financial as Ken Barnes remember:

'The years we reached Wembley, we were on £18.00 during the season and £12.00 in the 'close season'. Because the Final was in May it was classed as 'close season' so in '55 we took home £10 17/6 after tax. There was no bonus for just getting to Wembley although we did make a few bob from our Cup Final magazine. In '56 we got a bonus of £20 for winning! Looking back, I was fortunate because I played in two Cup Finals when a lot of great players never played in any.'

To Roy Paul, the money meant very little: 'I am very proud, and so is the team to be taking the Cup back to Manchester. I know we will have a great reception.' After the game he gave the match ball to his son: 'Never lose that, son. It was the ball that won the Cup for your Dad.'

Even the pain was worth it to Bert Trautmann: 'The pain stabs right through me but it's worth it. I don't care if the pain's like a red-hot poker I know I've got that Cup medal in my wallet.'

Manchester was ready for a party. The victory parade was covered live from 6.45pm to 7.30pm by Granada Television's outside broadcast cameras. The team was due at London Road at 6.19pm before travelling to the Town Hall via London Road Station approach; Piccadilly; Market Street; Cross Street; Princess Street to Albert Square. The team was due at the Town Hall at 6.50pm for a civic reception with 500 people representing sport, civic and trade chiefs.

Roy Paul lifts the Cup in jubilation. Bert Trautmann, on the right, looks less happy, with his head tilted at an acute angle.

The drama of the Cup Final had reached its climax with the Cup being paraded through the streets and, after the Civic Reception, the players slipped away for a well-earned break. For Bert, however, events were about to take a turn for the worst. Still in acute pain, he was recommended to see an osteopath in St Anne's Square.

The osteopath carefully examined Bert's neck and then began to manipulate his vertebrae. As he worked on the his spine, Bert was almost passing out with the pain. The torture continued as the osteopath started forcing his head backwards. Unable to stand the searing pain any longer, Bert screamed out for the treatment to stop.

Returning home, Bert was now in total despair and was finally driven to Manchester Royal Infirmary, where an X-ray quickly revealed the problem. A vertebrae had been pushed out of alignment, crushing several nerves and was fortunate that his mauling at the hands of the osteopath had not finished him off.

Bert was immediately admitted to hospital to have corrective surgery, which involved bolting callipers into his cranium to support his neck and spine.

By now, news had reached the press and the hospital was besieged by journalists desperate for a scoop. Bert's future as a footballer was routinely written off – no player could recover from such an injury. The situation, as we know, turned out somewhat differently but, whatever the personal outcome for Bert, he was now a national hero and the events of the Cup Final had taken on a new meaning. The 1956 Cup Final would forever be remembered as the 'Trautmann Final' with its most memorable moment the great goalkeeper being helped unsteadily off the pitch having won one of football's greatest honours.

The manager and the players

In all, just 12 players took part in the FA Cup run, only one of them, Jack Dyson, not having featured the previous season.

Les McDowall – The Manager

Born 25 October 1912, Gunga Pur, India, Appearances 117 League, 6 FA Cup, 20 Reserves, 1 Lancashire Senior Cup, Other 8. Goals 9. Playing career John Neilson School, Glentyan Thistle, Kilbarchan Athletic, Unemployed X1, Sunderland 1932, Manchester City 1938, Wrexham player-manager 1949.

The son of a missionary, Les received training as a draughtsman but joined the ranks of the unemployed early in the 1930s. After he had played 13 League games for Sunderland in almost 6 years, he joined City for £7,000. The Second World War came along and suddenly Les's talents as a draughtsman were in demand. In addition he played 122 wartime games for City, scoring 8 goals, and also guested for St Mirren, Rangers, Partick Thistle and Morton.

He won a Second Division championship medal in 1947, went to Wrexham as player-manager two years later, and applied successfully for the City post a year later. In his first season at Maine Road, the team won promotion. He was a quiet, thoughtful man, never afraid to experiment with new plans. The 'Revie Plan', based on the Hungarian national side's style of play, took the club to the FA Cup Final in consecutive seasons. Less successful were the 'Marsden Plan' and a later one which consisted of filling the side with wing-halves! After City were relegated in 1963, Les became manager at Oldham Athletic for two seasons and then left football. He died at Northwich in 1991.

Billy Spurdle

Born 28 January 1926, St Peter Port, Channel Islands. Appearances 160 League, 12 FA Cup, 69 Reserves, 5 Lancashire Senior Cup, 2 Manchester Senior Cup, 14 Other. Goals 49. Playing career Oldham Athletic (amateur in WW2, pro 1948), Manchester City 1950, Port Vale 1956, Oldham Athletic 1957.

Evacuated to Lancashire just 24 hours before the Germans occupied the Channel Islands in 1940, Billy Spurdle joined Oldham Athletic from where City boss Jock Thomson signed him in 1950 for £12,000. Initially City were not too sure what his best position was and he appeared in both the wing-half berths, as well as in various spots in the forward line. In 1951 Billy represented 'The Rest' against Wolves, the League champions in this annual fixture and in 1952-53, he was joint top scorer with Johnny Williamson, each player putting away 11 goals. He was later tried as a right-winger, a role in which he excelled. Billy played in all the early rounds of the 1955-56 cup run but everybody felt the utmost sympathy for him when he was forced to miss the Wembley date through a painful attack of boils. He had played in the losing final the season before and was the first Channel Islander to appear in a Cup Final. A move to Port Vale followed before he rejoined Oldham, playing a further 144 League games for them and scoring 19 goals. He retired in 1963 and, four years later, returned to Guernsey to grow tomatoes and do some coaching.

Bert Trautmann

Born 22 October 1923, Bremen, Germany Appearances 508 League, 33 FA Cup, 4 League Cup, 36 Reserves, 3 Lancashire Senior Cup, 2 Manchester Senior Cup, Other 53, Playing career St Helens Town 1948, Manchester City 1949, Wellington Town 1964.

A former paratrooper, Bert came to England as a prisoner-of-war and was placed in a camp at Ashton-in-Makerfield. He played for St Helens Town – eventually marrying the manager's daughter – and came to Maine Road at first as an amateur at a cost of £550 amid protests from Jewish groups in the city. However, the players made him welcome and he soon proved his worth as a successor to the great Frank Swift. The number of times that Bert stood between City and a sound thrashing were innumerable as the team went through some traumatic times in the early 1950s. He seemed to save his most brilliant performances for games in London. He played in both the Wembley finals in 1955 and 1956, ending the second game with what was later diagnosed as a broken neck. In April 1964 he was given a testimonial game at Maine Road when around 50,000 people turned up to pay tribute to him. It was a great shame that West Germany never recognised his ability with international caps simply because he played out of the country, but he did captain the Football League here in 1960 versus the Irish League. After leaving City, Bert played a few times for Wellington Town then managed Stockport County for a spell. He later became a much-travelled coach, working mainly in Africa and the Far East. Today, he is always accorded a great welcome when he comes to watch City in action from his retirement home in Spain.

Ken Barnes: 'It took a while for him to settle because a number of people had a go at the club for employing a German. However he was a good lad and took the stick. There have been lots of great keepers over the years but if there's been anyone better than Bert I'd love to have seen him.'

Roy Clarke: 'By far the best goalkeeper I've ever known, probably slightly better than Frank Swift who I played with and against, and that's saying something. What made Bert different was that he turned defence into attack quicker than any other goalkeeper. Unlike many keepers, he could catch and throw the ball in one movement, and when he threw the ball out to you it would be in the direction you required, so you'd be running onto the ball. In first class football that meant a great deal in terms of space and time for the person receiving it. He was also a great shot stopper.'

Bill Leivers

Born 29 January 1932, Bolsover. Appearances 250 League, 20 FA Cup, 11 League Cup, 98 Reserves, 5 Lancashire Senior Cup, 3 Manchester Senior Cup, 26 Other. Goals 8. Playing career Chesterfield 1950, Manchester City 1953, Doncaster Rovers 1964 (player-manager), Workington 1965.

Bill joined City for £8,000 from Chesterfield. He was a gritty, no-nonsense defender who tackled hard but fairly. His debut was at Preston at the start of the 1954-55 season when the Revie Plan was unveiled, but he lost his place to Jimmy Meadows. He came back into the team in November 1955, having worked hard to improve his game, and became the regular right-back. He won a Cup winner's medal the following spring and he represented the FA against an Army X1 the same year. Ever-present in the League side in 1956-57, he overcame a cartilage operation in 1960 and returned to the team as a central defender. He moved on in 1964 as player-manager with Doncaster Rovers, taking them to the Fourth Division championship in 1966 and later he managed Cambridge United, Chelmsford City, and Cambridge City. He is now retired.

Roy Clarke: 'A very tough strong footballer who knew an awful lot about the game. He bragged about what he would do to his opponents! Because of his size he wasn't the quickest but read the game really well. Bill and Roy Paul used to go at it hammer and tong with their opponents, but there was never any animosity, they were just hard tacklers doing their job.'

Bert Trautmann: 'He talked very tough about what he would do to his opponents but that was it. He had a lot of room to cover because Ken Barnes would often be attacking, so when moves broke down he had to cover two players. He was a great team player, wasn't the most skilful but could read the game well.'

Roy Little

Born 1 June 1931, Manchester. Appearances 168 League, 18 FA Cup, 87 Reserves, 6 Lancashire Senior Cup, 1 Manchester Senior Cup, 30 Other. Goals 3. Playing career Greenwood Victoria, Manchester City 1949, Brighton & Hove Albion 1958, Crystal Palace 1961, Dover FC (player-manager) 1963.

Roy Little, master of a clean tackle and also of accurate distribution, occupied the left-back berth in City's two mid-fifties Wembley trips. He will never forget his first senior City outing. The occasion was also an FA Cup tie, at home to Swindon Town in January 1953. The Blues enjoyed a stunning 7-0 win with Johnny Hart scoring four times. The following week Roy was retained in the side for his League debut against Liverpool at Anfield. His overall play was praised as City won 1-0. He was popular with his colleagues for his ability to raise a laugh even when times were not so good for the team. Brighton paid £4,850 for him in 1958 and he later spent two years with Dover as player-manager before returning north to work in the motor-auction business. Roy later became ground superintendent and steward of the Manchester University sports complex in Wythenshawe, as well as serving on the committee of Wythenshawe Amateurs FC. Today he is retired and is deeply involved in the City Former Players Association.

Roy Clarke: 'Roy was a full back of the first degree. Sharp, quick, good tackler and quick on the turn. Not many wingers got past him. He was a controlled player and could read the game well. He was a great personality and funny, a real friendly guy.'

Bert Trautmann: 'A very tenacious player, once he had his fangs into an opponent, he wouldn't let go. A great man-marker, he stuck to his opponents like glue.'

Dave Ewing

Born 10 May 1929, Perth Appearances 279 League, 22 FA Cup, 1 League Cup, 118 Reserves, 4 Lancashire Senior Cup, 1 Manchester Senior Cup, 36 Other. Goal 1. Playing career Luncarty Juniors, Manchester City, Crewe Alexandra, Ashton United.

Another player who appeared in both the Finals of the mid-fifties, Dave Ewing coined among the fans the phrase, "Pull up at Dave's," one that sounds like an advert for a transport cafe but which was in reality a tribute to his defensive qualities. His reserve and league debuts were against Manchester United, both formidable tasks, yet he came through them well. Many fans would say that his finest hour was at Wembley in 1956 when, realising that Bert Trautmann was seriously hurt, Dave shielded him as much as possible and kept the Birmingham City forwards away from the keeper. The great sportswriter Eric Todd once said of Dave, " … a player who can create a realistic impression of a man whose chief objective is to beat his own keeper without actually achieving it – well, not every time." The last comment refers to the fact that Dave holds the unenviable record of having scored the most own goals for the club, but at least he was in there battling. He later became a City trainer then a coach at Sheffield Wednesday, the manager at Hibernian and a coach at Crystal Palace. He returned to City until 1980 when John Bond dispensed with his services in favour of his own men. Sadly, Dave died in 1999 after a long illness.

Roy Clarke: 'A true stopper centre-half, great in the air, strong tackler, not that skilful but could kick a ball into the back of the stands when necessary. If we needed to waste time, he couldn't half waste it! He had a reputation of being a real hard man. If you took Dave on it was like running into a brick wall!'

Bert Trautmann: 'He had one of the biggest hearts in the game. When things weren't going too well and you were under pressure he was a tower of strength; you couldn't have a better player. The best example was at Wembley in '56 after I was injured. I remember twice going for a centre when he dived in to the rescue. People used to say 'Bert you saved us a point in such and such a game' but I disagreed because without David we wouldn't have held firm. Many times when we won by a single goal, he secured the win and not my play. He was a pure stopper but not the greatest back-passer; in fact, the best saves I made were from David!'

Joe Hayes

Born 20 January 1936, Kearsley Appearances 331 League, 24 FA Cup, 8 League Cup, 98 Reserves, 5 Lancashire Senior Cup, 2 Manchester Senior Cup, 36 Others. Goals 204. Playing career Kearsley West Youth Club, Bury (trial), Bolton Wanderers (trial), Manchester City 1953, Barnsley 1965, Wigan Athletic 1966, Lancaster City (player-manager) 1967.

Former colliery and mill worker Joe Hayes, who died in 1999, was one of Manchester City's most prolific scorers, top marksman in two of his City seasons, and the first player to score 100 goals for the club after World War Two. Turned down by both Bury and Bolton, he arrived at Maine Road with his boots wrapped in brown paper and asked for a trial. After a successful outcome he then asked for bus fare back to Bolton! His first team debut was at Spurs just two months after he signed for the Blues, and he rapidly became a regular in the side. Joe revelled in the introduction of the Revie Plan and showed wonderful ability to run onto through balls provided by either Revie, Ken Barnes or Bobby Johnstone and, in the 1956 Final, he scored City's opening goal after only 3 minutes after a build-up by Revie and Roy Clarke. Joe played twice for the England under-23 side, scoring a goal against Scotland, and also represented the FA. He also scored City's first ever goal in the League Cup competition. In 1964, he tore knee ligaments at Bury, an injury that not only sidelined him for 17 months but also marked the decline of his career. After his last links with the game had been severed when he left Lancaster Town, Joe worked for a finance company and then opened his own greengrocery business.

Ken Barnes: 'A great goal scorer for City. If there were twelve people in the box stopping him the ball would still end up in the back of the net. He was a patient and sharp player who had the knack of being in the right place when it mattered to stick the ball away.'

Roy Paul

Born 18 April 1920, Gelli Pentre, Wales. Appearances 270 League, 23 FA Cup, 1 Reserves, 38 Other. Goals 10. Playing career Ton Pentre Boys Club, Ton Pentre, Swansea Town 1938, Manchester City 1950, Worcester City (player-manager) 1957, Brecon Corinthians (player-manager), Garw Athletic (player-manager).

Raised in the coal-mining valleys of South Wales, Roy Paul – one of 12 children – made his first team breakthrough with Swansea Town in wartime football. He joined the Royal Marines as a PT Instructor, served part of the time during the war in India, but also turned out 84 times for the Swans. He also guested for Watford and Cardiff City. Along with other star players, he went to Bogota in Colombia to play for FC Millionaros, but refused to stay there as they would not take on board his friend, Everton's Jack Hedley. He was disciplined by the FA on his return for going without permission. City decided that he would just the man to lead their charge back into the First Division, and what an excellent investment Roy was at £19,500. The Blues went up, he played in both the mid-fifties cup finals, and international honours continued to come his way. In all he won 33 Welsh caps, 24 of them with City, and he also played for Wales against the Rest of the UK in 1951. His life style didn't go down to well at Maine Road; Roy loved a drink, but trained extremely hard to counteract any excesses. He was hugely disappointment when the Blues lost the 1955 final, and he threatened the rest of the team with all sorts of problems if a similar situation arose the following year. Happily it didn't! While he was at Worcester City that club achieved fame by beating Liverpool in the 1958 FA cup competition. When Roy finally hung up his boots he worked as a lorry driver but, sadly, today suffers from poor health.

Roy Clarke: 'Recently there was a vote on who had been Manchester City's greatest ever captain and Roy Paul won. Roy led by example, if an opponent had the ball he tackled … bang', his timing was perfect. He never gave into anybody; he stood firm. He always looked after his team-mates; if anyone took advantage of us he was there to look after us. Roy Paul used to come in ten to three; he'd get stripped straight away, bounce the ball and say, 'Come on, ****'. He used to have a go at anyone standing in front of the mirror, the toilets, the shower room … he'd just get the ball, bounce it … 'right, out we go'. That was it … he was the skipper.'

Bert Trautmann: 'Roy Paul was an exceptional footballer. He might not have been the fastest player around but he could read the game brilliantly. The best centre half and skipper we've had, an amazing man.'

Ken Barnes

Born 16 March 1929, Birmingham. Appearances 258 League, 23 FA Cup, 2 League Cup, 117 Reserves, 9 Lancashire Senior Cup, 3 Manchester Senior Cup, 32 Other. Goals 26. Playing career Moor Green, Birmingham City (amateur), Stafford Rangers, Manchester City, Wrexham (player-manager), Witton Albion (player-manager).

City shelled out a mere £900 for Ken Barnes, the player known popularly in his playing days as the 'best uncapped wing-half in the country'. In his first four seasons at the club he was selected for just one League game, at home to Derby County in January 1952, but his position was cemented in the first team with the introduction of the Revie Plan in 1954. He had helped to operate it successfully in the reserves during the previous season with Johnny Williamson. His skilful passing was a joy to watch, and he opened up many a defence to make chances for the City strikers. The nearest he got to international honours was to be named as a reserve for England against Wales in 1957, although he did represent the Football League. He remains the only City player to scored a hat-trick of penalties in a league game, against Everton at Maine Road in December 1957. He was later appointed City skipper for two seasons before moving to Wrexham as player-manager in 1961. He left a managerial position with Bangor City and returned to Maine Road as trainer-coach in 1970 and later became Chief Scout, unearthing priceless talent for the club's youth team. He retired in 1992 with a testimonial against Manchester United.

Roy Clarke: 'He was an ideal combination with Roy Paul because Roy had a defending quality, Ken an attacking one. Ken was brilliant at seeing an opportunity and delivering the ball. He didn't score many but got up to support the attack. He had a lot of skill, imagination and was a good reader of the game. He was also a right character; he used to hang a carrot on your peg … 'donkey!' … I can still see it now.'

Bert Trautmann: 'It has been said about many players that they were the best in their position not to play for their country. Well, in our day, Ken Barnes was such a player. Ken was a key player in our style of play, he would see me coming out for a cross and turn and go for the open spaces. A great team player.'

Bobby Johnstone

Born 7 September 1929, Selkirk. Appearances 123 League, 14 FA Cup, 12 Reserves, 1 Manchester Senior Cup, 19 Other. Goals 60. Playing career Selkirk, Newtongrange Star, Newtongrange Bluebell, Hibernian 1946, Manchester City 1955, Hibernian 1959, Oldham Athletic 1960, Witton Albion 1965.

Son of a well-known Scottish amateur footballer, Bobby Johnstone was one of the Hibernian forward line, every one of whom was an international. In the nine years Bobby was with the Edinburgh club, they won three Scottish championships and were also runners-up three times. City boss Les McDowall showed what a shrewd judge of players he was when he signed Bobby for £20,700 in 1955, and as if to celebrate his arrival Joe Hayes scored a hat-trick against Bolton Wanderers in a 4-2 home win. The wee man had gained 13 Scottish caps prior to joining City and he was to receive another four while with the Blues. He also represented the Scottish League 6 times and played for Great Britain against the Rest of Europe in 1955. His ball control was a sheer delight to watch and his football brain was second to none. City fans were wondering who was going to lose his first team place to accommodate Bobby, but that problem was solved when poor Johnny Hart, a most popular player, broke his leg at Huddersfield in the next game after Bobby's debut! Johnstone holds the distinction of becoming the first player to score in successive cup finals. He hit a ten-yard header into the net in the 1955 final and the following year he scored City's third goal by hitting a stinging drive past Birmingham's Gil Merrick. Bobby spent a brief spell back in Scotland and then joined Jack Rowley's Oldham side, scoring 35 goals in 143 League outings. He did not play for Witton Albion after joining them owing to a troublesome knee problem and, in 1978, went to Workington as manager as well as running a local youth side, Mount Pleasant. In later years Bobby was employed by a scaffolding firm and as a part-time driver. He devoted a great deal of time to playing bowls, a sport he loves, went back to Scotland, and this year returned to the north-west.

Roy Clarke: 'An inside forward, Bob was a playmaker who could play on crutches! His football brain was like lightning, he would stand and direct the whole forward line from the centre circle; he was such an intelligent player. Also what pace he had, he'd knock a ball out and be moving, shouting 'hold the ball … hold the ball', then he'd go 'now' and you'd give it to him. He was sheer class; he'd receive a ball … look … and was gone.'

Bert Trautmann: 'For a small player to establish himself in our day he had to be a good footballer. Bobby read the game brilliantly, was a great distributor of the ball and technically he was the perfect footballer.'

Jack Dyson

Born 8 July 1934, Oldham. Appearances 62 League, 9 FA Cup, 77 Reserves, 3 Lancashire Senior Cup, 1 Manchester Senior Cup, 7 Other. Goals 54. Playing career Oldham Athletic (amateur), Nelson, Manchester City 1952, Stirling Albion 1961, Oldham Athletic 1962, Northwich Victoria 1963.

Part of Jack Dyson's early City career was spent on National Service but he will always remember his first season involved with the first team. He scored a goal on his league debut away at Bramall Lane in October 1955 against Sheffield United and ended the season by scoring the Blues' second goal in the 1956 Cup Final against Birmingham City. He was to an extent a victim of his own success. A cricketer with Lancashire CCC, he was required at certain times of the year by both the County and by Manchester City, which was a great shame as it meant that he could not devote all his attention to either sport. He also suffered from injuries. In 1957 he broke a leg in the annual pre-season practice game at Maine Road, then the same thing occurred the following season at Barrow in a Lancashire Senior Cup tie. City had paid Nelson the grand sum of £25 for Jack, and he moved to Stirling Albion for £2,000 in 1961. He stayed there for two seasons and also played cricket for Forfarshire, but his footballing days ended sadly as he was firstly suspended by Stirling for breach of contract and then sacked by Northwich for failing to attend training. After he finished playing he had a variety of jobs, including working for a spell in City's Commercial Department. He now lives in the Oldham area.

Roy Clarke: 'Jack Dyson was brilliant at any sport, a natural ball player, he even opened for Lancashire at cricket. Before a game his hands would be white … he was so nervous. It's hard to understand why because he was such a skilful ball player with great ball control.'

Roy Clarke

Born 1 June 1925, Crindau, Newport. Appearances 349 League, 20 FA Cup, 51Reserves, 7 Lancashire Senior Cup, 4 Manchester Senior Cup, 36 Other. Goals 115. Playing career Albion Rovers (Wales), Cardiff ATC, Cardiff City, Manchester City, Stockport County, Northwich Victoria (player-manager).

Roy Clarke not only won 22 Welsh international caps (and also played in a Victory International in 1946) but he was also capped as a schoolboy for his prowess in baseball! When City paid out £12,000 for him in 1947, he set a record. His last game for Cardiff City was in Division Three South; his first appearance for the Blues was in Division Two; and his next one, thanks to promotion, was in the First Division. He was a brilliant left-winger who could turn defences inside out and was an expert in crossing the ball. Even when the Blues went through an extremely poor season in 1949-50, Roy emerged as top scorer … with 9 goals! He was bitterly disappointed to miss the 1955 Cup Final through a knee injury, especially as he had scored the winning goal in the semi-final against Spurs at Villa Park, but he got another chance and played the following year against Birmingham City. Roy joined Stockport County for a spell and then took up the reins at Northwich Victoria, but he left to concentrate on his sports outfitters business before rejoining the Blues as organiser of the Development Association. In 1966 he again took up managership, this time of the newly-built Social Club at Maine Road, a job he did with distinction until 1988. The club won awards for the quality of the entertainment it provided. Today he can often be seen at the ground and is heavily involved in running the City Former Players' Association.

Ken Barnes: 'Determined, tricky and fast, a classical winger with the aim of getting to the dead ball line to pull the ball back across the face of the goal. Could score and make goals, and turn a game. He was a brave player because in our day a full back could put you into the track and that would be it!'

Don Revie OBE

Born 10 July1927, Middlesbrough. Appearances 163 League, 15 FA Cup, 13 Reserves, 2 Lancashire Senior Cup, 25 Other. Goals 56. Playing career Archibald Road School, Newport Boys Club, Middlesbrough Swifts, Leicester City 1944, Hull City 1949, Manchester City 1951, Sunderland 1956, Leeds United 1958.

Don Revie only made two appearances in City's 1955-56 cup campaign, one of them in the final, as he had been in dispute with the club and the manager, Les McDowall, for much of the season.

Having played in the 1955 final, this one should have completed a hat-trick for him, but he had missed out on Leicester City's Wembley visit in 1949 due to severe nosebleeds. The Blues had tracked him for nearly two years before he eventually signed, and he had long spells at wing-half as well as playing as an inside-forward. Then McDowall introduced the so-called Revie Plan, requesting that Don fulfil the role that Johnny Williamson had done so well in the reserves.

So what was basically a 4-2-4 formation took the field with Ken Barnes as the other link man between the defence and the forwards. As both he and Don were excellent passers of the ball, many chances were created for the front-runners to tuck it away into the net. He was selected for the England B team, received 6 full England caps, and represented the Football League twice. In 1955 he became the first City player to be named Footballer of the Year. In 1955 he was suspended by the club for missing training, and a year later the board insisted that he re-sign for City before touring Australia with a footballing party. After two years with Sunderland Don moved to Leeds United where he eventually became manager. They were not a popular side with other fans, accusations of over-physical play being bandied about, although their success under Don cannot be denied. From 1974-77 he managed England and then shocked the football world by walking out to coach in the United Arab Emirates. He was only 61 when he died from motor-neurone disease in 1989.

Ken Barnes: 'A deep thinker, his movement off the ball was brilliant. A great long passer, he could place the ball on a three-penny bit. He had great vision, wasn't clever at beating people but when it came to using the ball intelligently he was fantastic. Always easy to find, if a player was in trouble he'd be available; a great footballer.'

Bert Trautmann: 'I looked for Don Revie most of the time because, when he came deep, he always found space. He would have his back to an opponent when I had the ball and because he knew how I threw, would immediately spin round knowing the ball would end up in front of him, then he could go forward and distribute it. He was also an expert at the 'banana' pass or shot, really pinpointing them.'

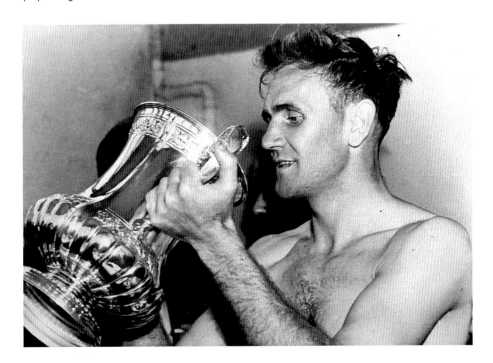

Bert Trautmann: A Tribute

*"There have only been two world-class goalkeepers. One was Lev Yashin
and the other the German boy who played for Manchester – Trautmann"*

Lev Yashin

I t is a favourite game of football fans – putting together a team of the greatest ever players. Would Stanley Matthews and Tom Finney be automatic choices or Bobby Moore and Bobby Charlton? Younger fans might scoff at the mere mention of players they never had the good fortune to see, after all football today is supposed to be a faster and tougher game; but those who stood on the terraces in the 1950s and 60s remember as a Golden Age the days when they stood shoulder to shoulder in their thousands every Saturday afternoon to lose themselves in the magic of the simple game. Every team had their stars, often local men from the same working-class backgrounds as the supporters – men who would catch a bus or tram to the ground and whose take home pay was little more than those who came to watch them. Sir Stanley Matthews expressed his opinion when asked whether he resented the huge wages paid to footballers today, No, he reflected, all he could remember was his astonishment at being paid for doing something he loved best.

They were different times so, perhaps it is fatuous to choose an all-time great team but had you asked fellow professionals in the 1950s who they would choose to guard the net, the answer would have been unanimous. In Stanley opinion "there is no doubt he was one of the world's great goalkeepers." Tommy Docherty went one step further: "he had everything you look for in a world class goalkeeper. I still get asked today who was the best goalkeeper I have ever seen. It's about opinions, but I think he might just be the best ever." Opponents were undivided in their praise: Jackie Milburn thought that "he had the quickest reflexes I have ever experienced and he was a bloody nice bloke as well" whilst to Bobby Charlton he was simply "the best goalkeeper around at the time."

What is astonishing about these tributes is that they were paid to a player who never achieved international recognition and whose reputation was established solely on the league grounds of the English First Division, playing for a team whose form was generally a source of exasperation for its loyal supporters. Even more remarkable is that he first had to win over supporters in the face of adverse criticism over his nationality.

When one thinks about Bert Trautmann, one image immediately springs to mind, the 1956 Cup Final and his broken neck. Dramatic and sensational as that was, it somehow overshadows and dilutes the man's ability – his sheer presence, lightning reflexes, magnificent hands and temperament. Equally important to his team was the ability to make a save, read the situation in front of him and set up an attack with his immaculate use of the ball from his own goal area.

Bert's courage and temperament should, perhaps, be put in the context of his wartime experiences, which are another story. When Bert left school, he became an apprenticed motor mechanic and played his early football as an aggressive centre forward for his local team Tara FC. By this time, Germany was at war and Bert was recruited into the forces and was transferred to the parachute regiment, acquiring his 'wings' in 1941. His first action was on the dreaded Eastern front where the massive German advance across Russia had become bogged-down at Stalingrad. As the suicidal efforts to defeat the Soviet forces became more and more prolonged, fighting units were transferred to counter the threat from the West and one of Bert's abiding memories of the horror and carnage of war was at Arnhem, when an Allied Airborn Division was dropped into an area occupied by the German forces. The drop was into a wooded area and soldiers were left hanging by their parachutes in the trees completely at the mercy of the German infantry who picked them off at leisure.

As the war was entering its final phase, the German Army was retreating in disarray leaving pockets of troops abandoned and exposed to the Allied armies. Bert and a colleague, a long way from their base, were picked up by an American contingent and stripped of their weapons. Two 'Yanks' were designated to escort them to one of the PoW centres. After walking miles with their hands in the air, Bert eventually turned to speak to their escorts and found that they had disappeared. The pair was eventually picked up again and shipped to England. Thus began his life in PoW camps, finally ending up in St Helens.

Today, we now have over two hundred foreign players in the Premiership. Back in the early post-War years, few teams would have considered signing anyone from outside of the United Kingdom, so the idea of a big blonde German ex-soldier signing for one of the country's top clubs was headline news. Bert had been playing football for an English club, but St Helens Town were in the Lancashire Combination and the issue of his selection at that level was not controversial. St Helens had been attracting the attention of numerous league scouts but no one was rushing in to sign the club's greatest talent. His transfer to City during the 1949-50 season was therefore a surprising decision by City, in spite of their desperation to find a goalkeeper capable of replacing the legendary Frank Swift. Manchester had a large Jewish community, many of them City fans. One could hardly expect them to enjoy the spectacle of an ex-German paratrooper competing for their acclaim.

Protests were inevitable and the pressure on Bert must have been unbearable when he made his league debut against Bolton at Burnden Park. Chants of 'Heil Hitler' and 'Nazi' greeted him as he took his place between the sticks and, although he personally had a good game, the Wanderers finished up winning convincingly 3-0. Bert recalls: 'My first game for City was against Bolton. Frank Swift called everybody 'son' and came over to me before the game, 'You're playing your first league game, son. When you go out, ignore the crowd completely, they're not there ... play for yourself ... just concentrate'. Even in later years I took that advice with me. Sometimes people thought I was a bit high-handed but I was simply concentrating. In the dressing rooms before a match everyone prepares in their own way; I was no different. I always tried to get my circulation going twenty minutes before kick off and would put my right boot on first; also I would never wear a darned sock! When I went out, I just put my head down, threw my cap in the net and that was it. I knew fans were there, I could hear them, but you had to stay apart.'

The next week, Bert was to play his home debut against Birmingham City and faced an anxious week as more anti-German sentiment was expressed. Fortunately, a local rabbi made an appeal for tolerance, insisting that Bert could not be held personally responsible for the crimes of the Nazi regime and wished him well in his sporting endeavours. Remarkably, the home match passed without serious incident. Bert, greatly relieved by the crowd's encouragement was in excellent form as the Blues cruised to a 4-0 victory. When asked recently whether the 1956 Cup Final was his favourite memory as a City player, Bert replied that his home debut was the match he considered the most emotionally important. The fact that he, a German, could be accepted so readily by the City supporters meant everything to him.

Bert went from strength to strength in his first season, more than could be said for a lethargic City who were frustrating their masochistic fans who turned out in incredible numbers (nearly 60,000 for a February match against Middlesbrough) to watch a team bent on relegation. One match sticks out. Bert's London debut against Fulham was played against a background of anti-German taunts. To Bert, the match had an added importance. 'My father-in-law told me you hadn't achieved anything until you were recognised by the London press. He told me the papers in

Manchester had a certain amount of power but were nothing compared to the ones down south. My first game in London was against Fulham; Arthur Rowley was their centre forward. We lost by one but it could have been eight, it was one-way traffic; I don't know how I kept some of the shots out. All the papers praised my performance. At the end of the game both teams spontaneously lined up in the tunnel to applaud me. Remember I'm a Jerry, I was at the River End and had to walk through them all. I couldn't believe it.'

Bert's first season was a personal success but for the club it had been a bitter disappointment. The second division was not an attractive option, even at that time, and in time honoured fashion manager Jock Thompson was shown the door. His successor, a former City player Les McDowall, had no track record as a manager but, as events turned out, proved to be an inspired choice.

Football in England was still wrapped up in the complacent belief that, as inventors of the game it was still well ahead of the rest of the world in skill. So complacent, in fact, that invitations to enter the first three World Cups were contemptuously rejected. The early 1950's registered its first seismic shock when a strong England team was beaten by the United States to be followed two years later by their destruction by the great Hungarian team at Wembley. Thinking footballers realised a revolution was needed to bring the English game into the modern world. Training for most clubs consisted of running round the pitch, a bit of circuit training and, perhaps, a game of head tennis. Tactics were rarely discussed, managers usually expected players to use their talents in the best way possible whilst on the pitch. Roy Clarke remembers his introduction to Manchester City: 'I signed for City on the Friday after they clinched the championship in 1947. I was invited to their team meeting and sat in the corner; there were stars everywhere, including the great Frank Swift. The team was playing their penultimate game of the season and I thought I'd here amazing words of wisdom. The manager Sam Cowan walked in and picked up the ball. 'Hello lads', he bounced the ball on the floor, 'Okay, we're playing West Ham today … get stuck in', then walked out. I couldn't believe it!'

Continental methods were obviously superior and, fortunately, Les McDowall was prepared to test out new tactical approaches. Pre-season training started earlier, ball skills were paramount and the days of the long ball from defence were over. McDowall relied on Don Revie as the focal point of his new strategy and Revie revelled in his new role as receiver and provider of balls played to the feet.

There were set-backs, especially City's first game using the new tactics when an exuberant Tom Finney led Preston to a 5-0 victory, but persistence began to pay off as results began to run in City's favour. For the Blues patient supporters, these were halcyon days, culminating in a Cup Final appearance against Newcastle. For Bert, the Wembley appearance was the fulfilment of a dream. 'Germany became World Champions in 1954 and played against England in December that year. The German FA asked me to assist as an interpreter and the night before the match we went to Wembley to inspect the ground. I walked onto the pitch and asked if I could go into the goal. I stood between the posts and thought fancy playing here just once in your life. Six months later, I was back for the Cup Final against Newcastle; absolutely magnificent.'

In spite of the anti-climax of Cup Final defeat against Newcastle. Bert had proved his quality time after time and, with the rest of the team, looked forward to the 1955/56 team with justifiable optimism. As usual, the club flattered to deceive in the league, finishing a respectable yet disappointing fourth. The FA Cup was another matter – winning for Bert his only major football medal as a player. His courage that day in staying on the field whilst in great pain is one of the enduring moments in Cup history.

The season had one additional surprise for Bert when he became the first foreign player to win the coveted English Player of the Year. In five seasons, he had achieved universal recognition as the best goalkeeper in the game.

Sadly for Bert, and City's supporters, the 1956 Cup Final was as good as it got. Don Revie left for Sunderland as the Blues lost their way and drifted down the table. But leaving the club was not an option for Bert. He felt a tremendous loyalty to City and was prepared to play out his days for them. Sadly, his final season was marred by the parsimony of the club who, after the maximum wage was abolished, decided to pay other players in the team substantially more than Bert. Bert, who was on £30 a week in 1963, discovered that new signings were being paid more than double his wage.

Not one to shirk a confrontation, he asked the management for parity, after all his loyalty and commitment to the club. When told that no more money was available, Bert asked to be played in the reserves since he was obviously not highly enough paid to be in the first team.

So an era for Bert and City rapidly came to a close as he looked elsewhere for career options. Stockport County offered him his first management post followed by posts in Germany, Burma (as national coach), Tanzania, Liberia, Pakistan, Yemen and Malta. His work for the Burmese national team was particularly successful winning the gold medal at the 1973 ASEAN Games.

Bert has now retired to Spain but still returns regularly to Manchester when he meets up with other ex-City players. He is deeply committed to the club and this affection is reciprocated from the many Blues' supporters who hold him in such great respect. Perhaps the final word should come from City's captain on that great day in 1956. Roy Paul was asked who was the greatest goalkeeper and he replied:

"Only two come into the reckoning, both from Manchester City, Frank Swift and Bert Trautmann. Swifty had a knack of winning over a crowd by his antics. Bert had to win their approval by his daring and courage in the face of adverse criticism about his nationality. I have no doubt in my mind that Trautmann was the greatest goalkeeper I have seen – Bert would be my first choice."

Bert Trautmann reads about his Wembley heroics whilst recuperating in hospital.

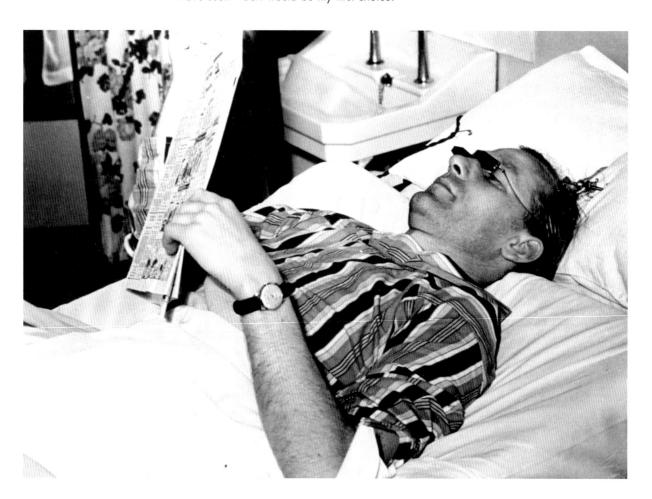

Manchester City Cup Kings 1956

FA Cup 3rd Round

Aldershot 1 Barnsley 2
Arsenal 2 Bedford Town 2
Aston Villa 1 Hull City 1
Bolton 3 Huddersfield 0
Bradford Park Ave 0 Middlesbro 4
Bristol Rovers 4 Manchester Utd 0
Bury 0 Burnley 1
Charlton 7 Burton Albion 0
Doncaster 3 Nottingham Forest 0
Everton 3 Bristol City 1
Exeter 0 Stoke City 0
Hartlepool 0 Chelsea 1
Leeds United 1 Cardiff City 2
Leyton Orient 1 Plymouth 0
Lincoln 2 Southend 3
Liverpool 2 Accrington Stanley 0
Luton 0 Leicester 4
Manchester City 2 Blackpool 1
Northampton 1 Blackburn 2
Notts County 0 Fulham 1
Portsmouth 3 Grimsby 1
Rotherham 1 Scunthorpe 1
Sheffield United 5 Barrow 0
Sheffield Wed 1 Newcastle United 3
Sunderland 4 Norwich 2
Swansea 1 York 2
Swindon 1 Worksop 2
Torquay 1 Birmingham City 7
Tottenham 4 Boston United 0
Walsall 0 Port Vale 1
West Ham 5 Preston 2
Wolves 1 West Brom 2

FA Cup Third Round Replays

Bedford Town 1 Arsenal 2
Hull City 1 Aston Villa 2
Scunthorpe 4 Rotherham 2
Stoke City 3 Exeter 0

FA Cup Fourth Round

Arsenal 4 Aston Villa 1
Barnsley 0 Blackburn 1
Bolton 1 Sheffield United 2
Bristol Rovers 1 Doncaster 1
Burnley 1 Chelsea 1
Charlton 2 Swindon 1
Fulham 4 Newcastle United 5
Leicester 3 Stoke City 3
Leyton Orient 0 Birmingham City 4
Liverpool 3 Scunthorpe 3
Port Vale 2 Everton 3
Southend 0 Port Vale 1
Tottenham 3 Middlesbro 1
West Brom 2 Portsmouth 0
West Ham 2 Cardiff 1
York 0 Sunderland 0

FA Cup Fourth Round Replays

Chelsea 1 Burnley 1
Doncaster 1 Bristol Rovers 0
Scunthorpe 1 Liverpool 2
Stoke City 2 Leicester 1
Sunderland 2 York 1

FA Cup Fourth Round Second Replay

Burnley 2 Chelsea 2

FA Cup Fourth Round Third Replay

Chelsea 0 Burnley 0

FA Cup Fourth Round Fourth Replay

Burnley 0 Chelsea 2

FA Cup Fifth Round

Charlton 0 Arsenal 2
Doncaster 0 Tottenham 2
Everton 1 Chelsea 0
Manchester City 0 Liverpool 0
Newcastle United 2 Stoke City 1
Sheffield United 0 Sunderland 0
West Brom 0 Birmingham City 1
West Ham 0 Blackburn 0

FA Cup Fifth Round Replays

Blackburn 2 West Ham 3
Liverpool 1 Manchester City 2
Sunderland 1 Sheffield United 0

FA Cup Sixth Round

Arsenal 1 Birmingham City 3
Manchester City 1 Everton 0
Newcastle United 0 Sunderland 1
Tottenham 3 West Ham 3

FA Cup Sixth Round Replay

West Ham 1 Tottenham 2

FA Cup Semi Final

Birmingham City 3 Sunderland 0
Manchester City 1 Tottenham 0

Final Manchester City 3 Birmingham City 1

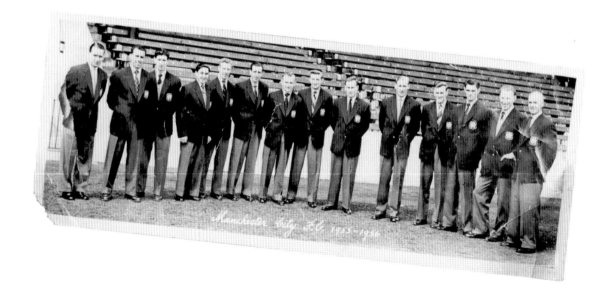

Manchester City F.C. 1955-1956